# Later Writings by Pilgram Marpeck and his Circle

## Volume 1:
### *The Exposé, A Dialogue, and Marpeck's Response to Caspar Schwenckfeld*

Anabaptist Texts in Translation

# Anabaptist Texts in Translation

Anabaptist Texts in Translation is a publication series sponsored by the Institute of Anabaptist Mennonite Studies (IAMS), located at Conrad Grebel College, in Waterloo, Ontario, and published in cooperation with Pandora Press. The aim of the series is to provide English-speaking readers with reliable translations of significant Anabaptist texts.

1. *Later Writings by Pilgram Marpeck and his Circle. Volume 1: The Exposé, A Dialogue*, and Marpeck's *Response to Caspar Schwenckfeld* translated by Walter Klaassen, Werner Packull, and John Rempel

# Later Writings by Pilgram Marpeck and his Circle

## Volume 1:
### *The Exposé, A Dialogue,* and Marpeck's *Response to Caspar Schwenckfeld*

Translated by
**Walter Klaassen, Werner Packull,
and John Rempel**

**With an Introduction by
John Rempel**

Published by Pandora Press
Kitchener, Ontario
Co-published with Herald Press
Scottdale, Pennsylvania/Waterloo, Ontario

Canadian Cataloguing in Publication Data

BX
4930
.M37
1999
v.1

Marbeck, Pilgram, ca. 1495-1556
  Later writings by Pilgram Marpeck and his circle.

(Anabaptists Texts in Translation, ISSN 1487-2447 ; 1)
Contents: v. 1. The exposé, A dialogue, and Marpeck's Response to Caspar
Schwenckfeld.
Includes bibliographical references.
ISBN  0-9683462-6-X (v. 1)

1. Anabaptists – Doctrines – Early works to 1800. 2. Theology, Doctrinal –
Early works to 1800. I. Klaassen, Walter, 1926-  . II. Packull, Werner O.,
1941-  . III. Rempel, John D. IV. Title. V. Series.

BX4930.M37 1999             230'.43             C99-931612-5

LATER WRITINGS BY PILGRAM MARPECK AND HIS CIRCLE.
VOLUME 1: THE EXPOSÉ, A DIALOGUE, AND MARPECK'S RESPONSE
TO CASPAR SCHWENCKFELD

Copyright © 1999 by Pandora Press
      51 Pandora Avenue N.
      Kitchener, Ontario, N2H 3C1
      All rights reserved
Co-published with Herald Press,
      Scottdale, Pennsylvania/Waterloo, Ontario

International Standard Book Number: **0-9683462-6-X**
Printed in Canada on acid-free paper
Cover design by Clifford Snyder

07 06 05 04 03 02 01 00 99 10 9 8 7 6 5 4 3 2 1

# Table of Contents

# Preface

This book inaugurates a series of what we envision to be many volumes of Anabaptist texts in translation.

The process of making Anabaptist texts available to wider audiences began in the last century, with the publication of scholarly, critical editions of sixteenth-century Anabaptist sources in Dutch and German. Many of these sources had languished in European archives for centuries before being published in splendidly annotated volumes. Some two decades ago, significant numbers of these sources began to appear in the English language. This was due particularly to the systematic publication of the translation series *Classics of the Radical Reformation* (Herald Press), a project that still continues.

As original immigrant languages fade in North America, increasingly replaced by English, translated historical texts become important links to the faith witness of the past. Those who may not have learned Dutch or German now have before them the words of Anabaptist faith parents. With a translation in hand, the possibility of establishing an intimate aquaintance with kindred sixteenth-century minds is only an arms-length away.

Many worthwhile small texts will never find their way into a *Classics of the Radical Reformation* volume. Our series, *Anabaptist Texts in Translation*, aims to publish such texts that, in spite of their brevity, nevertheless contribute significantly to our understanding of the Anabaptist movement.

This volume of writings by Pilgram Marpeck and his Circle is the first of a planned set of three, all making available previously untranslated writings. These smaller volumes may be considered appendices to the substantial collection translated by William Klassen and Walter Klaassen, *The Writings of Pilgram Marpeck* (Scottdale, PA: Herald Press, 1978). Besides the upcoming Marpeck volumes, further translation projects are currently in preparation which, we trust, will appear in this series in due course.

Special thanks go out to Walter Klaassen, Werner Packull, and John Rempel, who made this volume possible by the generous donation of their time, historical expertise, and linguistic skills.

Arnold Snyder
*Series Editor*                                   *Anabaptist Texts in Translation*

# Pilgram Marpeck:

## An Introduction to his Theology and Place in the Reformation

John Rempel

### The Mystery and the Man

Pilgram Marpeck was lost to the world for almost three centuries. Although he was a prolific writer, his wisdom disappeared almost without a trace. How could such a thing happen? Part of the reason lies in the insecure existence of dissident communities during the Reformation. They were repeatedly dispersed and had only rare access to the printing press, and persecution and dissension decimated congregations. What they were able to publish was often lost or confiscated. In addition, some of Marpeck's writing, particularly the *Response* to Caspar Schwenkfeld's critique of his views, pursued vast theological questions removed from the day-to-day struggles of a suffering church.[1] Since the *Response* and Marpeck's many letters were circulated in manuscript form, their visibility and influence were highly circumscribed. As the first generation of Anabaptist leaders and the theological issues for which they went to the ramparts receded, so did their writings.

The generation of leaders which followed Marpeck's entered a marginalized ministry, lived out on the edges of society. Whereas Marpeck and his generation contended for their convictions in the public square, their successors were more and more confined to obscurity. Increasingly, their energy was drained away from apologetics and mission to simple survival. To be sure, Marpeck's gifts were recognized by his followers during his lifetime. A circle of leaders, led by Leopold Scharnschlager, gathered around him, sharing the task of composing with him, then amending and circulating his writings for use by a second generation of Anabaptists. For instance, in the early 1550s twenty copies of the *Admonition* were carried to Moravia and read in all the sympathetic congregations there.[2]

In the third phase of his influence, beginning about 1570, aspects of Marpeck's thought and spirit were taken up – often without mention of his name – into certain South German and Swiss Mennonite communities.[3]

But soon after 1600, the trail to Marpeck grows cold.[4] Isolated handwritten manuscripts were passed on but there was no community left to champion them, with the consequence that his unique reading and practice of Anabaptism was lost as an identifiable form of thought and church order.

Two-and-a-half centuries later an auspicious discovery occurred. At the onset of a re-appraisal of Anabaptism in European Protestant historiography in the 1860s, a Marpeck manuscript was discovered in the Strasbourg Archive, only to be burned in a fire a few years later. Fortunately, parts of it had been handcopied, and those who had discovered in Marpeck a distinctive Anabaptist voice thus had scraps of evidence that the man no one knew had actually lived and written.

It was not until the 1920s that full texts of Marpeck's two major works, the *Admonition* and the *Response*, were rediscovered. They were a sensational find for Anabaptist studies. It was as if the lobotomy Anabaptism had endured with the loss of Marpeck's thought had been miraculously undone. Almost as sensational has been the ascription of authorship of significant additional works to Marpeck since the 1950s. These include *A Clear Refutation, A Clear and Useful Instruction,*[5] *Explanation of the Testaments,*[6] and the *Confession to Jan von Pernstain.*[7] At the same time, the examination of these works has led scholars to posit a collective authorship for some of them.[8] The attribution of the *Exposé of the Babylonian Whore* to Marpeck and of the *New Dialogue* to Marpeck's circle are of much more recent date. The case for their authorship is presented in this volume.

A voice and a movement which had disappeared have been recovered in almost full strength. It is a blessed irony of history that this forgotten man and his movement have spoken to the needs of twentieth-century Mennonitism as few of his contemporaries could.

## Origins and Early Ministry

Pilgram Marpeck was born into a devout Catholic family about 1495 in Rattenburg in the Tyrol. He learned the skills of a mining engineer and practised his profession in his native province. Some time before 1520 he married Sophia Harrer, and they became parents of a daughter, Margareth. By 1528, Sophia had died and Pilgram married again, apparently to Anna, who is mentioned in later correspondence. Pilgram and Anna adopted three children in Rattenberg but had no children of their own.

Marpeck began his public life at age eighteen in Rattenburg, when he was appointed by the city council to an administrative post in the local hospital. Eventually he held political office as a member of the Outer and then of the Inner city council of Rattenburg, was appointed mining magistrate, and even served a term as mayor in 1522.

During this period he was drawn to the cause of church reform through Lutheran influences. Then more radical reformers – notably Michael Gaismair, Leonhard Schiemer, and Hans Schlaffer – arose in the area and attracted Marpeck to their primitivist vision of a restored New Testament Christianity. A vibrant Anabaptist community emerged, including members of the mining guild. Requests by the authorities for Marpeck to aid in the arrest of local radicals led him to refuse the orders. The execution of Schiemer and Schlaffer, the most sophisticated and charismatic of the nonconformists, led Marpeck to resign his job.[9] As a consequence he was banished from Rattenberg.

Remarkably enough, Pilgram and Anna seem to have left their children behind in Rattenberg; nothing further is said of them. The parents became refugees, finding their way to Anabaptist congregations in Moravia. Oral tradition has it that Marpeck was commissioned by these people to go to Strasbourg to baptize.[10]

## The Strasbourg Years

Religious life in Strasbourg had already been shaped by religious reform before Marpeck's arrival there in the late 1520s. The influence of some dominant personalities reached the city. Erasmus was the most radical of those reformers who remained loyal to Roman Catholicism; a host of pastoral, theological, and political factors led others to defy its authority. The revolt against Rome had been initiated on the continent by Martin Luther, Andreas Karlstadt, Ulrich Zwingli, Thomas Müntzer, and Conrad Grebel, and was carried out by them and circles of enthusiastic and gifted colleagues they had won to their cause. Bucer, Melanchthon, and Hubmaier are only the most famous of these many colleagues. Luther and Zwingli soon allied themselves with regional rulers, creating a new synthesis of church and state. Partly from expediency, but more because of their emerging view of the church, the radicals renounced the unity of church and state, and followed various paths to the formation of free churches.

Radicalism was in the air in central Europe: it had spread like a windswept forest fire roaring across even treeless spaces in the woods. Müntzer was the most charismatic of the leaders of the Peasant Revolt, a brush-fire-like series of uprisings by the "common man." Within a year the Lutheran princes of the Swabian League had crushed it. Further north, Melchior Hoffmann began preaching the end of the godless, creating an apocalyptic expression of Anabaptism. At the other extreme was Schwenckfeld, a seeker after the kingdom through mystical inwardness.

The latter two were among the many dissidents who sought refuge from persecution in Strasbourg, the New York City of its age, on account of its willingness, briefly, to tolerate nonconformists who found no haven elsewhere. Bucer and his co-worker Capito were in the process of establishing reform in Strasbourg, borrowing greatly from Zwingli and Luther, but more tolerant than either. Michael Sattler, the guiding spirit behind the Schleitheim Confession, fled to Strasbourg to spread his missionary vision and to dispute with its Reformed leaders. His attack on the lack of binding and loosing in the mass church led to the incorporation of discipline as a mark and practice of the Reformed Church there. Representatives of various streams of restorationist Christianity came and went in that city, cross-pollinating in the process. As they followed through on their most coveted tenets, some allies became antagonists. Such was the case with Marpeck and Schwenkfeld.

When Marpeck arrived in Strasbourg in 1528, he was able to use his professional qualifications to fill the post of engineer of the city's forests. This role offered him safety and security, and the freedom to engage and influence the diverse expressions of the Radical Reformation to be found there. The first tumultuous phase of reform – both magisterial and radical – had spent itself. The initial outburst of Anabaptist vision in Zurich had been as much a defiance of papal and magisterial reform as it was a working out of the consequences of so decisive a break with tradition. Hosts of radicals had been imprisoned (and some killed) for the audacity of their faith. Many – like Hubmaier, Sattler, and Hans Denck – were stopped dead in their tracks in the midst of experiments to implement their convictions. Others, like the millennialist Hoffmann, were driven by persecution to become prophets of the world's doom.

Under the moderately tolerant Reformed regime of Strasbourg, dissenters from more brutal governments found refuge there. Various radical leaders gathered followers around them. Until the early 1530s Martin Bucer and Wolfgang Capito, the leading ministers of the city, allowed themselves to be drawn into disputations with nonconformists, without imprisoning them afterwards. What a difference that must have made to the spirit and substance of Anabaptist church life and theological reflection! The sixteenth century was an age full of passion and judgement, but these were tempered in places like Strasbourg by an acknowledgment of the humanity, and sometimes even the sincerity, of one's opponents. This was true between the radicals and the state church as much as among the groups of radicals.

Thus, the city suited Marpeck. He was an unusual radical, peace-loving by nature, steadily able to discern the difference between having the courage of one's convictions and demanding that kindred spirits think and act alike on every point. Like Christians everywhere at the end of the middle ages, Marpeck believed that Christ would soon return to judge the living and the dead. But he did not believe that the world was therefore damned and must be fled.

In Strasbourg Marpeck took his place as one of a second wave of Anabaptist leaders whose task it was to guide the movement beyond its explosive origins into ongoing communities. Although the comparison is seldom made, his career and role had noteworthy parallels to those of Menno Simons. Both spent their lives ministering to persecuted congregations and developing an apology for their existence. Both argued with magisterial reformers and with fellow radicals. Menno and the Dutch and North German congregations he oversaw faced persecution day by day; Marpeck's communities were less persistently hounded. So the challenges before them were different, as were their talents. Menno was a pastor with a soft heart but a fairly hard head. He believed that only by means of unrelenting dogmatic positions and stringent church discipline could Anabaptism survive. Even though he and his wife Gertrude found a safe haven later in their ministry, they represented a wilderness church whose calling increasingly became living "without spot or wrinkle" far from a fallen world.

In general, this was true of Marpeck's setting, but there were factors which became decisive for the different path he took. First were the circumstances. Marpeck was a public official as well as a minister. He worked with people who were both his potential persecutors and his friends. He had the disposition, time, and freedom to explore both what divided him from and united him with his detractors as well as his fellow radicals. For example, during his Strasbourg years Marpeck and his final antagonist, Caspar Schwenkfeld, shared elements of a common vision. Whereas Menno saw the inner moral life of the community as its Maginot

Line, Marpeck went on the offensive and set forth a theology of the incarnation as Anabaptism's first line of vindication. Both of them grounded the authenticity of Anabaptism in ecclesiology, its theology as well as its practice. They sought congregations of believers whose supreme goal was to live out the Sermon on the Mount. For Menno, church discipline was the lifeblood of this undertaking and theology a necessary evil. For Marpeck, it was the other way around.

Marpeck and Menno apparently neither met nor read each other's writings. Had they done so, Marpeck might have challenged Menno with some of the very charges he made against Schwenckfeld, because Menno shared the tendency of parts of Reformation radicalism to spiritualize sacramental and liturgical realities. To free themselves from the materialistic rut of popular Catholicism, many reformers mutilated the principle of the incarnation by internalizing sacramental reality. At the same time, the Anabaptists were distinguished by their belief in a visible church of believers as the literal body of Christ in the world. Thus, both the spiritualist and sacramentalist impulses were at work in Anabaptist thought. It was Marpeck, more than any other Anabaptist, who attempted a synthesis of both impulses.

**Theology**

As far as we know, Marpeck never studied theology in a formal way, either early in his life or in the course of his ministry. Yet he was an intellectual. He was an original thinker in so far as he saw the inadequacy of prevailing spiritualistic and apocalyptic trends among the radicals in his search for an Anabaptist view of the church enabling it to live in but not be of the world. To buttress this missionary ecclesiology he shamelessly borrowed from a variety of theological sources. Marpeck had a thirst for theological and moral truth, for grand principles as well as for their working out in the lives of believers. He was an autodidact, with the eclecticism which often accompanies that route to scholarly achievement. Loserth observes that even though Marpeck wrote in German, he thought in Latin, used Latin sentence structure, and wrote in the manner of Latin humanist stylists. He deduces that Marpeck had a scholarly education.[11]

Marpeck saw that "the hint half guessed, the gift half understood is incarnation" (T.S. Eliot). He realized that without a doctrine of God's redemption of history and matter, a visible church as the ark of salvation has no theological basis. Anabaptists saw their beleaguered fellowships as extensions of Christ's earthly presence, yet their anti-Catholicism prevented them from cogently re-interpreting the sacramental principle in a way compatible with a believers church ecclesiology. Without the sacramental principle, the objective reality of the body of Christ on earth was in danger. What remained was a subjective reality, the church as a human endeavour, ceaselessly striving for perfect holiness of life. This was the slippery slope onto which both Menno and the Swiss Brethren had been pushed by disposition and circumstance, contrary impulses in their theology notwithstanding. By the time Marpeck and Schwenkfeld squared off in the 1540s, Marpeck had come to realize that the lack of an explicit sacramental principle grounded in the incarnation led, in the case of the Anabaptists, to legalism and, in the case of the spiritualists, to otherworldliness. Both tendencies spelled the end of mission.

The congregations under Marpeck's influence had a distinctive interpretation of the role of the church at the end of the age. Marpeck was the shepherd of congregations which, though harassed, sought to make Anabaptist-inspired discipleship the everyday practice of everyday people; they were insecure and outcast but for the most part they were not on the brink of martyrdom. They resisted taking refuge in an apocalyptic view of the last things and the violent – or at least vengeful – interim ethic which often grows out of it. The language of the *Exposé of the Babylonian Whore* is spicy by our standards. But what makes it distinctive and remarkable is the counsel it proffers: "preach the gentle, humble Christ," "leave vengeance to God," "the Word of the Lord is the only judge and sword." Marpeck's kind of Anabaptists strove to be an advance party of the kingdom in ordinary time, as engineers and housewives.

There was a reason for the capacity to resist apocalypticism. It lay in Marpeck's belief about the incarnation. In Christ taking on flesh, God had befriended our mortal existence and used the things of earth to show forth his provision. Marpeck was convinced that not only individuals but the whole creation was redeemable. He believed that in Christ's incarnation God had come to us on our terms, "as a natural man for natural men." In his death Christ had triumphed over the devil and restored the potential of creation. Now the physical world, and with it the human mind and body, could transcend its "fleshly" nature and take on a "spiritual" one. The church was a "physical gathering" indwelled by the Spirit: outer and inner were part of a single reality. Both the church's worship and its obedience were sacramental actions, i.e., manifestations of God's nearness in everyday life.

Marpeck's special relevance to radical Christianity on the brink of the twenty-first century is his view that the Gospel brings about not only the rupture of fallen human existence but also the possibility of its restoration. God provides for the church to carry out its calling within time and makes the created order a latent means of grace. Marpeck sought a church which could provide sustenance for engineers and housewives, both when circumstances permitted them to carry out day-to-day responsibilities and when conscience compelled them to become outlaws. It was a tall order, but in Strasbourg, and then Augsburg, it could at least be worked on.

**Itineracy**

As the lines of reform hardened in the state church and among the radicals, life in Strasbourg became more precarious for nonconformists. Marpeck's dissent from the established church concerning infant baptism led to an expulsion order. Early in 1532 the Marpecks took up a twelve-year itinerant ministry. For parts of this time they disappear from view. Either because of endless pastoral challenges or because of outright persecution, Marpeck wrote little – or at least little of what he wrote has survived – until late in that period. It is likely that *A New Dialogue* is one of the few pieces dating from early in his itineracy. The *Dialogue's* set of questions and answers expresses Marpeck's persistence in the art of persuasion, and perhaps his confidence that Anabaptism would win the day.

The contest for primacy among different streams of radicalism heightened year by year. As the challenge of apocalypticism receded, that of Schwenckfeldian Spiritualism took centre stage. When the former threat retreated to the wings, Marpeck was audacious enough to enlist the thought of an apocalypticist, Bernard Rothmann, to confront the challenge of Spiritualism. In 1542 Marpeck edited Rothmann's *Admonition* by judicious cuts and expansion, and made it his own. Then, in 1544, he and his circle set to work on the first section of the *Response* to Schwenckfeld.

For parts of these dozen years the Marpecks travelled in Moravia and Switzerland. In Moravia they encountered Hutterianism. In the end, Marpeck concluded that its mandatory communitarianism made a law of something which the New Testament and the Holy Spirit consigned to freedom. In Switzerland their time with the Swiss Brethren impressed Marpeck with another form of legalism, that in which exacting conformity in all aspects of behaviour is required. His views are found in the letters he addressed to the Brethren.[12]

## Augsburg

By the time he completed the first part of the *Response*, Marpeck had resumed his profession in a new location, Augsburg, and was elder, or bishop, of a struggling Anabaptist congregation there, much as he had been in Strasbourg. Anabaptism had arisen in Augsburg in 1524 but was effectively suppressed in 1527. It re-emerged in 1533 and survived the upheavals occasioned by Catholic and Protestant parties warring for control of the city. Schwenckfeld resided there in 1534 and 35, leaving a following of sympathizers, some of whom were drawn from the ranks of the Anabaptists. Marpeck had sent the *Admonition* to an Augsburg Anabaptist, Helena von Freyberg, in 1542. It is likely that she passed it on to the Schwenckfeld circle and thence to the man himself.

Soon after his arrival in the city, the council hired Marpeck to manage the municipal forests and water supplies. As a resident and city employee he was exempt from local taxes and military service. Sketchy evidence suggests that his congregation experienced times of toleration alternating with spells of persecution. The times of toleration were long enough to permit sustained theological reflection by Marpeck, fellow leaders, and members at large. The precarious status of Anabaptists in Augsburg was a fact of life, but the clash between a state church and a free church was not the issue which preoccupied Marpeck or defined his theological engagement late in life. What preoccupied his mind and defined his thinking was the conflict between two schools of radicalism based on two, by now mutually exclusive, theologies and practices of church life. That followers of Schwenckfeld and Marpeck embodied competing versions of radical reform next door to each other added a raw edge to that debate.

The second part of the *Response* and the massive *Explanation of the Testaments* – the Biblical spade work for the expanding debate with Spiritualism – were written early in this era, as were many of the pastoral letters. The limited toleration of dissenters in Augsburg does not seem to have permitted any overt evangelizing. Thus, the baptism of new believers ceased to be an everyday occurrence and ceded its place as the flashpoint of debate and proclamation. It is arguable, from the straitened circumstances and altered profile of Anabaptists in the city and the prominence given to it in part two of the *Response*, that the Lord's Supper replaced baptism as the sustaining ritual of the congregation during this time. This conjecture would help to explain its centrality in the debate Marpeck carried on with Schwenckfeld in the *Response*. There the Lord's Supper assumes a definitive role, both as a dominical institution in its own right and as a prototypical theological case study.

## The Challenge of Spiritualism

A final factor in Marpeck's development – and in Anabaptist experience at large – is obvious enough to be overlooked. For Anabaptism the visible church was the extension of the incarnation in time. As Anabaptists understood the matter, Christ had commanded his church to meet and to follow his commandments, most especially that of loving worldly neighbours as well as fellow believers. The church could not forsake its visible form, its embodiment, without losing its identity. In Spiritualism this was not so. Since the body of Christ was thought by Schwenckfeld and those who shared his convictions to be the inner communion of true believers, visible community was a desirable but not essential reality of the Christian life. This was not only a conceptual, but a painfully existential, distinction between Spiritualists and Anabaptists – the latter being much more vulnerable to persecution. The different situation of the two groups in the world became as significant for their relationship to each other as the emerging theological differences between them.

Throughout the phases of his ministry, Marpeck retained and deepened the main impulses of his theology, but with one crucial difference between his early and late ministry. In 1528 the overwhelming challenge to Anabaptism had been a repressive state allied with an established church. The visions of reform among the diverse coteries of radicals at that time were as much complementary as competitive. By 1544 this order had been reversed. By then the threat to South German Anabaptism came from Spiritualism, a kindred movement. Spiritualism was uniquely dangerous to the theology developed by Marpeck, given its grounding in the incarnation. He was struck with increasing force by this truth just as his erstwhile friend and ally, Schwenckfeld, became convinced that Marpeck's incarnationalism was the most challenging of all expressions of Anabaptism to the mystical inwardness of Christ.

## Conclusions

All things considered, the enduring impression Marpeck left on Anabaptist (and indirectly, on Free Church) life was his rejection of the spiritualistic tendency in late medieval and Reformation thought. He was unable to shape the alternative he proposed with consistency, but his principles and many of his deductions from them stand. He rejected an ontological barrier between the worlds of spirit and matter. Following from this rejection, the pre-eminent goal of his theology was to create an apology for a visible church of believers. In order to do so, he focused the debate on ceremonies as manifestations of Christ's presence with his people. Marpeck taught that ceremonies were the point of intersection between the divine Spirit and human faith. He believed that external works were of one being with the inward reality they represented. He based this claim on the fact of the incarnation, and in turn, presented ceremonies as the ultimate demonstration of the incarnation. To do this he unfolded a christology and a trinitarian structure inspired by the Gospel of John.

The significance of mediating position precariously established by Marpeck's sacramental realism can be seen if it is cast into another set of categories, those of "Protestant principle" and "Catholic substance." The latter was the teaching of the incarnation as the rock from which ecclesiology had to be hewn. The former, especially in its radicalized form, was the claim that faith was the *sine qua non* of the church and the Christian life. Marpeck's attempt to bring both into a single reality was focused in his doctrines of baptism and the Lord's Supper.

Given Marpeck's remarkable synthesis, two riddles confront us. Why did his elaborately crafted union of inner and outer reality fall prey to internal contradiction? And, why did this singular figure disappear from history for three centuries? In my hypothesis, which follows, the two questions and their answers are related.

Marpeck retreats from his robust incarnationalism, most dramatically, late in the second part of the *Response*, just as he has completed the arduous task of marrying a believers church ecclesiology with the sacramental principle. My view is that Marpeck – or the collective of which he was the guiding spirit – was profoundly intimidated by Schwenckfeld's trump card, his teaching on the inwardness of Christ. Schwenckfeld argued in a way that made it seem the Anabaptists were defending a lifeless ceremonialism and a church to which the Holy Spirit was a stranger. Marpeck's retreat was more psychological than theological. He was willing to go to any lengths to prove that his was not a lifeless ceremonialism. Yet his theological grounding remained intact and he returned to it again and again.[13]

As for the second riddle, why did Marpeck disappear from history? In my judgement, the conflict between spiritualistic impulse and sacramental ecclesiology is native to Anabaptism, to the Protestant Reformation, and to

Christianity as a whole.[14] In Mennonitism, the tension between the two has never been resolved.[15] Its theology of the church as the body of Christ is clearly sacramental, yet its spiritual psychology prizes the inward and the disembodied as more real and more blessed than the outward and the embodied. It found Marpeck's synthesis too daring, and preferred to learn its lessons from mentors with a less resolute theology of the incarnation.

Marpeck is worth reading today, above all because he held these two realities together. His incarnational theology came to most profound expression in his teaching on the sacraments as the point of intersection between Spirit and matter, grace and faith. His thought provided an alternative both to the sacramental objectivism of Roman Catholicism, summed up in its doctrine of *ex opere operato*, and to the spiritual subjectivism of the sacramentarians and Schwenckfelders. Marpeck is an ecumenically significant theologian because he held together convictions which much of the church has separated through the centuries.

# Notes

[1] The *Response*, commonly referred to in German as the *Verantwortung*, circulated solely in manuscript form in the sixteenth century. Its only publication was by Johann Loserth, ed., *Pilgram Marpecks Antwort auf Kaspar Schwenkfelds Beurteilung des Buches der Bundesbezeugung von 1542*, [Quellen und Forschungen zur Geschichte der oberdeutschen Taufgesinnten im 16. Jahrhundert] (Wien: Carl Fromm, 1929), hereafter cited as *Response*. It is preserved in three manuscripts: in the Bavarian State Library in Munich, Signature Cod. Germ. 925; in the State Library, Olomouc, Czech Republic, Codex III, 19; and in the City Library of Zurich, MSS B 72. Loserth found the Zurich codex the most useful, on account of its marginalia and accompanying documents (Loserth, 48-49).

The text of Schwenckfeld's *Judicium* or *Judgement* (hereafter referred to as *Judgement*) of Marpeck is found on pages 169-214 of vol. VIII, 1927 of the *Corpus Schwenckfeldianorum*, ed. C.D. Hartranft and E.E. Schultz Johnson (Leipzig: Breitkopf & Haertel, 19 volumes, 1907-1961), hereafter CS.

The text of Marpeck to which Schwenckfeld responds is his *Vermanung* or *Admonition* of 1542. It was printed in the sixteenth century. There are two extant copies of this printing: British Museum, Signature 3908.a.1; Wuerttembergische Landesbibiothek. Its only modern publication was based on the second copy. It may be found in C. Neff, ed., *Gedenkschrift zum 400 Jährigen Jubiläum der Mennoniten oder Taufgesinnten 1525-1925* (Ludwigshafen: Konferenz der Sueddeutschen Mennoniten, 1925), 185-282, (hereafter *Neff*). This text was translated into English by W. Klassen and W. Klaassen, *The Writings of Pilgram Marpeck* (Scottdale, PA: Herald Press, 1978), 159-302, hereafter *Klassen & Klaassen*.

[2] S. Boyd, *Pilgram Marpeck, His Life and Social Theology* (Durham: Duke University, 1992), 145.

[3] Arnold Snyder pursues concepts from Marpeck and his circle which re-appear in later Swiss Brethren writings in "The (not-so) 'Simple Confession' of the later Swiss Brethren," parts 1 and 2, to be published in the *Mennonite Quarterly Review* (1999).

[4] Werner Packull identifies a date of 1622 as the last written reference to a community of Marpeckites, in *Hutterite Beginnings* (Baltimore: Johns Hopkins, 1995), 360.

[5] W. Klassen, *Covenant and Community* (Grand Rapids: Eerdmans, 1968), 36-43.

[6] Klassen & Klaassen, 555. Two copies of this published text exist, one in the Central Library of Zurich (MFA 139), the other in the German State Library in Berlin (BF 8370). The title page of the *Testamentserleüterung* (hereafter *TE*) or *Explanation of the Testaments* reads as follows:

> *Testamentserleüterungen./ Erleütterung durch ausszug/ aus Heiliger*
> *Biblischer schrifft, tail und/ gegentail sampt ains tails angehangen*
> *beireden/ zu dienst und fuerderung ains klaren urtails/ von wegen*
> *unterschaid Alts und News Testaments/ und ir beder suendtvergebung/*
> *Opfer/ Erloesung/ Gerechtigkait/ Gnad/ Glauben/ Gaist/ Folck/ und*
> *anderem/ so grundtlich/ lauter und nutzlich zue ersehen/ genant*
> *Testamentserleüterung.*

Loserth (38) adds the following data: Ohne Jahreszahl und Druckort. Oktavband mit 406 Bll. Text. Ausserdem 11 Bll. Enthaltend Titel, Vorred, und Register, "ueber inhalt der Capitlen und Summarien des Buchs." Zwischen beiden Paginierungen ein leeres Blatt.

[7] Boyd, 98-101.

[8] Jan Kiwiet makes the case for a "Gemeindetheologie," a congregational theology in which Marpeck was part of a collective in *Pilgram Marpeck* (Kassel: J.G. Oncken, 1957), 75. Most students of Marpeck have come to the same conclusion, arguing largely from external evidence – scattered written comments concerning Marpeck's collaboration with others. I argued the opposite case from internal evidence. I was struck by the fact that, at least the *Response*, has all the marks of an individual striving for the vindication of his reputation. See John Rempel, *The Lord's Supper in Anabaptism* (Scottdale, PA: Herald Press, 1993), 103 *et passim*. I am less convinced of my position than I once was, but have not yet read a contrary interpretation which accounts for the sense of wounded pride – more likely an individual than a collective trait – which permeates the *Response*.

[9] Boyd, pp. 21-41, ably traces the intellectual and social forces at work in Rattenburg and identifies evidence of their influence in Marpeck's later writings.

[10] Packull, 135-38 and Boyd, 52 both offer interpretations of data concerning this obscure phase in Marpeck's ministry.

[11] Loserth, 1-2.

[12] The extant letters are found in Klassen & Klaassen, 303-554. Heinold Fast has been at work for years on a definitive critical edition of the *Kunstbuch*, which contains not only all of Marpeck's known letters, but also numerous writings from various members of Marpeck's circle. While the writings of Marpeck contained in the *Kunstbuch* have been

translated (in Klassen & Klaassen), the remaining *Kunstbuch* writings stemming from Marpeck's circle have not. A future volume in this series (Anabaptist Texts in Translation) is planned that will present these writings of the Marpeck circle in English translation.

[13] This approach may be seen in eucharistic section of the *Admonition* (Klassen & Klaassen, 273ff) and the *Response* (Loserth, 559ff). In both cases Zwingli and those with similar views are evoked. But in neither instance is this line of defence at the heart of Marpeck's argument. Since Marpeck took over the substance of Rothmann's position, the problem is not only Marpeck's but that of the relationship in Anabaptism between ecclesiology and pneumatology. See my treatment of the matter in Rempel, *Lord's Supper*, esp. 126-42.

[14] See J. Jungmann's treatment of the spiritual and material dimensions of reality in the ancient church, in *The Early Liturgy* (Notre Dame: University of Notre Dame, 1959), 114ff.

[15] See my "Christian Worship: Surely the Lord Is in this Place," *The Conrad Grebel Review*, 6 (Spring 1988), 101-17.

# Exposé of the Babylonian Whore

[Attributed to Pilgram Marpeck]

Translated
with an introduction
by
**Walter Klaassen**

# Introduction

Recent bibliographical research has demonstrated that Marpeck's *Exposé of the Babylonian Whore* was printed in two editions, of which only one copy of the first and two copies of the second have survived. (For a full discussion, see item 5 in the literature list below.) The earliest edition of the *Exposé* has now been shown to have been published at Cammerlander's press in Strasbourg around 1531, just before Marpeck's expulsion from the city. Typographical evidence strongly links this earliest edition to Pilgram Marpeck, for it is typographically identical to Cammerlander's printing of two of Marpeck's tracts, both published in 1531, namely Marpeck's *A Clear Refutation* and *A Clear and Useful Instruction*. The only known copy of the Strasbourg edition of the *Exposé* is found in the Landesbibliothek Stuttgart.

A second edition and print of the *Exposé* has been shown to have been published sometime in the 1540s in Augsburg, at the press of Philip Ulhart. Again there is a connection with Marpeck, for Marpeck resided in Augsburg from 1544 until his death in 1556, and Ulhart printed several of his writings. Two copies of this second printing have survived, one in the Stadtbibliothek Augsburg and the other in Munich. Hans J. Hillerbrand published a facsimile of the Augsburg copy in the January 1958 issue of the *Mennonite Quarterly Review*. This translation has been prepared from the Hillerbrand facsimilie.

Neither Hillerbrand nor other scholars who analyzed it made serious attempts to identify the author of the anonymously published *Exposé*. In an essay on that subject published in 1984, Walter Klaassen identified the author as Marpeck, a claim that has been bolstered by the subsequent bibliographical and typographical research of Adolf Laube, Helmut Claus, and others, as summarized above. The same typographical evidence argues for the inclusion of the anonymous *Dialogue* in this collection of materials written and published by Pilgram Marpeck and his circle. A translation of the *Dialogue* follows the *Exposé* in this volume.

The historical setting and date of the first edition of the *Exposé* can be determined from internal evidence. Marpeck is addressing, indirectly to be sure, his erstwhile Lutheran co-believers who had prepared themselves for armed resistance against the Emperor Charles V and the Catholic princes to defend the reform. The theological justification for military resistance was worked out by the Lutheran theologians in June 1531. The Schmalcaldic League of Protestant princes and cities had already been formed earlier that year. References to the Lutheran readiness to defend the Gospel with the sword are very immediate, referring to events transpiring at the time of writing. The booklet, which bears no date, could therefore have been written and published early in 1532. (For a full discussion of the date, see items 4 and 5 in the list below.)

The tract is one of the best Anabaptist statements on how Christians should relate to the divinely appointed authority of secular government. Christians, Marpeck argues, have no right to claim the benefits of government, such as protection of property, and at the same time reject its divinely given right to rule. The Emperor is appointed by God and must be obeyed whether he rules justly or not – specifically, whether he attacks the Gospel with the sword or not. Christ calls his own to suffer the injustice without retaliation. But Christians do have an obligation to admonish the governing authorities to govern justly.

The "whore" whom Marpeck is exposing here is the claim of the "so-called evangelicals" (his term), by which he means the Lutherans, that opposing the Emperor with military might is an expression of the will of Christ and His Spirit. They claim that it is so because they are obeying Christ's command to love the neighbour by protecting that neighbour with the sword. Marpeck replies that love of neighbour can never justify harming another person for whom Christ died. The only sword given to Christians by Christ by which evil is resisted is the sword of the Spirit, the Word of God.

Evidently just before the manuscript was delivered to the printer, Marpeck remembered several other arguments from Scripture which would strengthen his case. He added them at the end rather than integrating them into the text. They have been designated in the translation as notes 1 and 2.

The *Exposé* is described and discussed in the following literature:

1. Hans J. Hillerbrand, "An Early Anabaptist Treatise on the Christian and the State," MQR 32 (January 1958), 28-47.

2. James M. Stayer, *Anabaptists and the Sword* (Lawrence, KS: Coronado Press, 1972), 170-72.

3. Werner O. Packull, *Mysticism and the Early South German-Austrian Anabaptist Movement 1525-1531* (Scottdale, PA: Herald Press, 1977), 150-55.

4. Walter Klaassen, "Investigation into the Authorship and the Historical Background of the Anabaptist Tract *Aufdeckung der Babylonischen Hurn*," MOR 61 (July 1987), 251-61.

5. *Flugschriften vom Bauernkrieg zum Täuferreich (1526-1535)*, Band 2, ed. Adolf Laube, Helmut Claus, et al. (Berlin: Akademie Verlag, 1992), 1036-39.

6. Werner O. Packull, "Pilgram Marpeck: *Uncovering the Babylonian Whore* and Other Anonymous Anabaptist Tracts," MQR 67 (July 1993), 351-55.

In the translation below, folio numbers of the original document are given in square brackets in the text as, for example **[A. ii v]**.

# Exposé of the Babylonian Whore[1]

Exposé of the Babylonian Whore and
Antichrist; its mystery and abomination
old and new. Also concerning the victory,
peace and rule[2] of the true Christians, and
published to show in what manner they obey
the authorities, and bear the cross of Christ
without rebellion and resistance, with
patience and love to the glory of God,
and to assist, strengthen, and
perfect all the faithful
and those who inquire
after God.

Matt. 22 [:21][3]
*Give to Caesar what is Caesar's and
to God what is God's*

Prov. 24 [:21]
*Have nothing to do with the rebellious*

May God give his grace toward true understanding for all who sincerely seek the truth in this last and perilous time. This time has now come, according to the word of the Lord in Matt. 24 [:11-12]. It says that temptations so difficult will come that it is possible that even the elect would not escape them unless the days were shortened. Lord, come; cut them short soon for the sake of your chosen ones. May your will be done soon.

Since the evidence of our eyes, our experience, and the witness of Scripture which sufficiently discloses itself through the action and favour of God, and which is now also understood through the events which are everywhere unfolding according to the Word of the Lord, all of God's creatures should tremble and be afraid of the stern judgement of God on his awesome day which is to come (Isa. 24 [:21ff.]; Jon. 2 [:?], 3[:4], Zeph. 1 [:7-18], 2 [:2], 3[:8]). The fact that the ruined, sodomitic,[4] perverted, abandoned, and seductive world does not comprehend this nor show any fear means that the Scripture in the Lord's Word is even now being fulfilled where it says that in the time of Lot and Noah they ate and drank, married and gave in marriage without any alarm, until they were altogether destroyed (Luke 17 [:26-30]).

Already the world overflows with the evil that once lay hidden in the mystery of wickedness. This mystery[5] is now being exposed through her own shame, just like a secret adulteress who for a long time deceived her husband under a false cloak of pious faithfulness and has now quite brazenly gone public. She has assumed all the wiles of a whore in order to seduce and deceive others with her thousand-fold cunning and skill. The whole world is now full of error and seduction, and all generations on earth are drunk with the wine of fornication, Rev. 18 [:3]. Only a few [Aiir] are shocked and have struggles of conscience from which the pure fear of God and true insight flow.

Although the great power of God is revealed and is now made manifest in the little flock in all its weakness, the villainous whore has, as always, not hesitated to make unclean and to defile that glory by means of many temptations and errors which emerge from the heart of the community of the faithful. They [the purveyors of error], however, are not of us as John says in 1 John 2 [:19]. But right there the whore is active with many false teachings and her own inventions to spy out our freedom according to the words of Paul in Gal. 2 [:4]. Blessed are those who are not stained nor polluted with this whoredom for they have been bought with the blood of the Lamb as firstfruits, Rev. 14 [:4], and rescued through the power of the Lamb, for the Lamb is the lord of Lords, and all the called, chosen and faithful ones are with him, Rev. 17 [:14], to whom alone be glory from everlasting to everlasting. Amen.

It is not really necessary to speak against the red Roman Whore now exposed.[6] For a long time she masqueraded as though she were married to the great spouse and bridegroom Christ. In this way she deceived and seduced both herself and others with her fornication. For the just and legitimate spouse and bridegroom Christ is now expelling and condemning her and all her strumpets, and is betrothing and marrying a new people[7] to himself through his cross, blood, and tribulation as is now evident. But it is the sign of the time that the serpent with her cunning is using new stratagems in her clever and tenacious mutiny against the true and spotless bridegroom Christ, as he has said. But our bridegroom has overcome the world and all its wickedness with his cross and death (John 16 [:33]). In him we will overcome and conquer in all things under the cross, in the simplicity of faith.

In order that the deceitful Whore and serpent with all her children and strumpets should perceive, know, and apprehend that a genuinely guileless faith can [Aiiv] detect all of her more recent insidious and deceptive tricks, as well as her customary malice which she plies against the children of God, I have decided to describe them and also to present an alternative. I am urged to do this as follows by a sense of obligation, to the praise of God, and for the service and strengthening of the faithful. May the Lord give his grace.

First, once the dragon and old serpent (Rev. 20 [:2]), who for a long time had concealed himself in the pretence of being the spouse and bride of Christ and deceived the whole world, became aware that his time was near, he in the dispensation of God revealed himself in part through his own prophets as though he was sorry for the colossal errors and apostasy of the Christians.[8] These prophets changed and made more attractive the great mystery of wickedness in the appearance of godliness, especially through the artifice of Scripture by which people are easily deceived. They presented infant baptism and the pope's idolatry [the mass or Lord's Supper], over which they quarrelled, and prattled about receiving it in both kinds *sub utraque specie* [in both kinds, the bread and the wine], as the most important matters on which their salvation depended, and so filled the whole world with their contentions and writings.[9] Thus Satan could carrry out his seductions so much the better. In Martin Luther's eyes all who eat and drink both the body and blood of Christ, regardless of whether they are adulterers or prostitutes, gluttons or drunkards, gamblers, murderers, betrayers, tyrants, deceivers, or whatever else are all a good community of his kind of godliness. Even as, in Luther's view, the body of Christ is in the bread and the blood in the chalice, his faithful ones and disciples are transformed into the nature and essence of Christ. For everything a person eats changes from its natural essence into something else; even so, should not their natures be changed into the nature and essence of Christ? As the teaching is, so also is the fruit.[10] Even as Luther and his followers persuaded the common people valiantly to defend the Word of God, all the while whitewashing that defence with Scripture [Aiiir] so that they were prepared to give life and limb for it, so now they induce the Princes, the nobility, and the cities to resist the Emperor.[11]

Woe to us because of the great bloodshed which God will bring upon all because of the false prophets and their supporters, as can be seen even now (Jer. 6, Ezek. 22 [:3-4], 23). May the Lord lead his own out of their troubles; may they not strike back, but remain under the cross and shadow of his wings in true patience (Ps. 17 [:8], 57 [:1]). For the Lamb of Christ[12] must suffer and be killed until the end of the world (Luke 17 [?], Rev. 13 [:8]). Pilate, Herod, Annas, and Caiaphas will unite against it as they united against the head (Luke 23). Christ was subject to all Authority[13] and never responded with violence. Even so today we must not resist. We will give the Emperor what is his and God what belongs to God (Matt. 22 [:21]). For the Authority has power over all temporal things except over vengeance which belongs only to God and never to man (Rom. 12 [:19], Heb. 10 [:30]). I know of no other Authority specifically appointed by God than the Emperor; all emperors hold the imperium even today and will hold it until the appointed time of which Daniel speaks (Daniel 11 [:36]), when the wrath of God shall come over the whole world (Isa. 24 [:17-21]). For all flesh needs his authority and rule.

But Christ does not distribute earthly inheritance or imperium. His own, whether they are treated justly or not, requite and repay with patience and love. All external things including life and limb are subjected to external authority. But no one may coerce or compel true faith in Christ, for it is concerned not with temporal but eternal life. This neither God nor any creature in heaven nor on earth can take away (Rom. 8 [:38-39], Matt. 10 [:28]). All true Christians have this faith, and that is why they are not concerned about their earthly life (Heb. 11 [:13-14], Luke 10 [:41-42], Col. 3 [:1-3]). Many are demonstrating this today, God be praised.

To sum up, I present to the so-called evangelicals[14] and their teachers and preachers no other alternative than the crucified, patient, and loving Christ. [Aiiiv] Whoever does not preach Christ but rather preaches the opposite is against Christ, regardless of whether he is an old or a new pope or Antichrist. Even if they were to preach as skillfully about God as Christ himself, it will not help unless they preach the gentle, humble Christ who can be known only under the cross, patience, and love. Whoever is not thus taught and so learns, no matter how evangelical he is, will interrupt Christ at the Judgement and say: "Lord, did we not drive out devils, prophesy, preach, eat and drink in your name?" Christ will answer: "Depart from me, you evildoers, I do not know you" (Matt. 25 [:41-44], Luke 13 [:26-27]). I could wish that those who avoid the strait gate of the cross of Christ and teach others to avoid it would read and understand the judgement of Christ more closely. Unless they have no faith at all, they should be very alarmed, for surely this judgement fits the new evangelical preachers and their followers more precisely than anyone else.[15] They do in part speak the truth about Christ, but they don't want to go through the narrow gate (Matt. 7 [:13-14]), because for carnal reasons they pressed the sword into the hand of the common people, dressing it up with scriptural teaching. According to Jude, those who resisted [Moses] perished in the uprising of Korah. At the present moment they[16] hide behind princes, cities and nobles, and incite them to follow the way of Cain by which they are submerged in error through the instructions of the prophets of Balaam. With much greater and more awful bloodshed than in the Peasant War, they will all perish in the rebellion of Korah, which is not the same as dying for Christ.[17] May the Lord lead his own out of such rebellion.

I give them testimony that I came to the truth partly through their writing, teaching, and preaching, for I was deeply possessed and imprisoned by the human laws of the papacy which is nothing but demon possession [Aivr]. Through their teachings and writings I was set free to the liberty of the flesh.[18] Where before I had been bound and had suffered in conscience, I was now free. I ate and drank with these teachers before the Lord as I then understood it, and thought that they preached a splendid Christ. In this new freedom I vigorously opposed the papacy with all the writings that helped me in that task as long as they agreed with the understanding, which was true, that it is not what goes into a man that makes him unclean, but what comes out of his heart (Matt. 15 [:10-11]). Confession and other papist rules and human inventions, which were not so easy to fulfill but did not have the true spirit of Christ, I readily accepted. Indeed the teachings in and of themselves were not wrong. But then as now the evangelical teachers said nothing about the mystery of the cross of Christ, and the narrow gate through which the flesh and the one who has been liberated from the Babylonian captivity could once again be led into the liberty of Jerusalem. On this there is silence. Not only that, but those who announce and teach it are persecuted by these teachers, who become their betrayers and executioners. For this reason they are justly called those workers of evil whom Christ banishes from his presence (Matt. 7 [25:41]). They teach the truth and the Gospel partially and point to the true way like a wooden hand at the fork in the road. What is missing in their teaching is the cross of Christ; they resist it and teach others to resist it. They take refuge behind princes, lords and cities although patient endurance, which alone triumphs over all tribulation, must be learned only under the cross. Christ the Lamb will be victorious (Rev. 17 [:14]), and not the lion, bear, wolf, dog, and leopard who gnash their teeth against each other and threaten to devour each other [Rev. 13:2].

Woe and alas for the teaching and kingdom of the Antichrist which now appears everywhere and which must be revealed (2 Tim. 3 [:1-9]). Discern and hear, all who have eyes and ears. Who are the deceivers and rebels, the Lamb of God [Aivv] or the cruel beasts? Children of God, have nothing to do with factions, do not be led astray, don't wish evil on your enemies, but heartily desire that good may happen and be done to them. You have only one judge, and he is in heaven. If the Authority, established by God (Rom. 13 [:1]), bears the sword in accordance with God's bidding and command, you are physically under the protection of God. When that Authority does not bear the sword as it should, but rather protects wickedness, destroys godliness, loves the lie, and persecutes the truth, you must be content to admonish that Authority, which is God's servant, to be converted and leave vengeance to God. No other sword or deterrence has Christ commanded his own to use. Whoever teaches the contrary is an Antichrist, liar, and deceiver (1 John 4 [:20], 2 John). He who looks for Christ elsewhere than under the cross in patience will not find him, no matter how many crucifixes and wooden hands there may be at the crossroads. The living cross and hand of Christ shows the way, does not stand immovable in one place, never has and never will, for it is itself the way from which the truth comes and is the truth from which life comes. This life comes from faith and faith gives birth to all virtue and the knowledge of Christ. For this is life eternal, that they know you, Father, the true God, and Jesus Christ whom you have sent (John 17 [:3]). The knowledge and teaching of Christ is not the life of the flesh, that distinct character[19] which we bring with us, but rather a new birth from God. The heritage of flesh and blood cannot remain after the new birth has taken place; it must die and come to nothing, for the person who wishes to save the first life and all that belongs to it will lose it, and whoever loses it will keep it for eternal life (Matt. 16 [:25], 19 [:29]). It is not very complicated; one needs only to bend one's back, freely offer it to the cross of Christ following our Lord Christ (Luke 9 [:23]), and faithfully bear that cross with gentleness, love, and patience as God's lambs (Matt. 11 [:10:16]). This cross-bearing is the resistance to the enemies of Christ by which we

[Bir] easily win, not the earthly but the eternal victory (Rom. 8 [:37], 1 John 5 [:4]). For this reason Christ says: "Rejoice! I have overcome the world" (John 16 [:33]). Earthly victories are short-lived; someone stronger comes along and nullifies them, and himself rules. Therefore it is not the victory of Christ but of the defective flesh, and will also disappear with the flesh. Wherever the true Christ rules in doctrine and life, all fleshly control comes to an end.

Likewise, where the physical, fleshly rule is established, Christ's rule is over. He is forced to leave the area and jurisdiction of the Gadarenes (Matt. 8 [:34]), because of the temporal loss [suffered by the owners of the pigs]. It was altogether an illegitimate business, and the loss should have been accepted for the sake of the salvation of the two men who were possessed by a legion of the Enemy through his manifold evil cunning. These two represent divine and fraternal love which have for a long time been seized and thwarted by Satan through selfish possessiveness.[20] Now we see these two who caused such great injury, and from whom no one in the world even today is safe, liberated by Christ and following him.[21] When the Gergasenes[22] suffered a small loss of temporal property which should have been endured for the love of God and the neighbour, they asked Christ to leave immediately, for they preferred the injury of selfish possessiveness even though it seduces and torments the whole world, and through which the love of God and the neighbour is thwarted and possessed [by the devil]. Christ yields and departs, injustice takes over and love grows cold (Matt. 24 [:12]). Self-seeking and uncontrolled domination injure whoever passes such a place. How great is the injury caused by this self-seeking through its demon-inspired senseless ways which destroy the whole world! But they would rather tolerate it than the godly, loving Christ who liberates those who are caught in the devil's power and injury. Woe to the blind Gergesenes, indeed to the whole world! [Biv].

Satan seeks to mix temporal power with Christendom by making it attractive through his prophets. These say that the godly must be protected (even though by saying this they actually injure them). Who, they argue, would desire to be a ruler if his subjects did not help him to preserve his power in order to protect the godly from the ungodly? No one would be safe in such a world![23] Thus they prefer godly Christians to be magistrates rather than someone from the world, and persuade many upright hearts that they should render to the government their sworn duty to maintain justice with arms and defiance, and in the disguise of Christ,[24] even though it is motivated by nothing but self-seeking.

I will certainly grant the point that all who claim to own something and desire protection for their property call on the government and complain that it is obligated to protect their temporal property and everyone else's in temporal peace [are right to do so]. For governments and their subjects have their source in this generation preoccupied with its own self-centredness.[25] The churches of Christ, however, do not have their birth in the self-centredness [of the flesh]; they come from Christ and are subject to him. Everyone is obligated to obey his own authority; the spiritual in spiritual peace, the carnal in carnal peace. The spiritual in Christ are committed to obedience to the Father in patience and love through the Word even as Christ, the Righteous One, became obedient unto death. The carnal are committed to preserving the power of the sword for punishment and vengeance against all wickedness, otherwise there would be no peace in temporal things as one can see everywhere. But it all flows from the goodness and mercy of God who knows all things and who desires only good for man and never evil. Even as God has offered peace to everyone, but not all have accepted it, likewise he has in his mercy also established and ordained divine Authority on earth to preserve temporal peace wherever the true peace of God, which is incompatible with self-seeking, is not accepted, in order that they don't destroy each other over their property. [Biir] Neither good governments nor subjects are to blame for this, but those who are evil. God permits it all for the sake of the good to prevent the even worse situation of total destruction in temporal things. Because of this goodwill and love of God for everyone, all true Christians are, as God's children, obligated by love to obey and be subject to all temporal authority even to death, but to give to God what belongs to him (Matt. 22 [:21]). Wherever the word and honour of God is assailed they are to act against the Authority, remain faithful to God, and surrender bodily life in patience and love to the government as the Authority over the flesh but not over the Word and the Spirit. Likewise Peter was commanded by the Lord to pay the tax (Matt. 17 [:27]), for our peaceful God desires only peace for everyone both spiritually and physically.

These are the weapons and the knighthood of the true Christians as Paul writes in 2 Cor. 10 [:4-5] and signs of the faithfulness of the eternal God. Moses was given the sword to enforce the moral laws so that peace would be preserved among the children of wickedness. Likewise Joshua and David and others were appointed to administer the punishment of God upon the children of wickedness, but only to preserve temporal peace through which the fleshly Israel was held together in unity.

But the office (*Amt*) which Christ and his own have is different from that of Moses. They neither have nor desire the peace of the body which was necessary then, but rather the peace of Christ who admonished them to have peace with each other. "Peace I give to you; my peace I leave with you. I do not give to you as the world gives. Do not let your hearts be troubled" (John 14 [:27]). The world does not know this comfort of God's Spirit, which is why it knows nothing about the peace of the heart. This peace does not complain about temporal persecution, however cruel it may be. No one had this peace before Christ who first redeemed us into this peace. His bodily departure was necessary, otherwise the Comforter would not have come (John 16 [:7]), so that we may endure all temporal tribulation in this peace of the heart without [Biiv] objecting. These, and not the comfortless complainers who accuse each other before men, are the true Christians. Christ is their true judge and Lord, for he will judge the whole circle of the earth (Acts 17 [:31]). Christ thus has a greater commission than Moses (Heb. 3 [:3], 8 [:6], 2 Cor. 3 [:7-8]). Under it no one will be accused through the law, nor will anyone accuse anyone else through the law.

Whenever Moses accuses or judges by the law, Christ is of no use. Christ spoke to the Jews who did not believe in him concerning this point in John 5 [:45]: "Do not think that I will accuse you before the Father; your accuser is Moses, on whom you have set your hope." Christ and his own are not accusers either in spiritual or in bodily matters; they are believing, loving, patient and gentle hearts. To such believers he says in John 8 [:31-32]: "If you continue in my word, you are truly my disciples; and you will know the truth, and the truth will make you free." This liberty of Christ is lord of all and all creatures serve her, although she does not rule but serve (1 Cor. 9 [:19-23], 10). For Christ the highest Lord did not come to dominate, coerce, condemn, nor rule. He will allow no one to be accused before him, and himself accuses no one. Rather, he was himself a servant, and allowed himself to be dominated, violated, accused, condemned, and cursed, and to suffer injustice.

That is our mirror in which we can see whether we have the stature of Christ or not. [If we acted like that] the strife about government would soon be laid by. It is argued that Abraham, Jacob, Moses, and David also had the Spirit of God, and even so bore the sword against the wicked, and that whoever had the Spirit of God also had the Spirit of Christ. That argument is the work of Satan who tries hard to confuse the making of distinctions[26] in order to preserve his glory and kingdom. At that time, in the counsel of the faithful God who knew fallen humanity's tendency to strife, there could be no peace unless carnal fear [Biiir] kept them in check from Cain and Abel onwards (Gen. 4). The spiritual peace of Christ could not come until Christ had purchased it through his departure in the flesh. When he said "consummatum est," he brought all carnal rule to an end (John 10 [19:30]). He rules in his own through his Spirit alone also in temporal matters, and distinguishes the spirit of the accusing, vengeful Elijah from the Spirit he gave to his own. Through his Spirit they were born; through that Spirit they are still being born. When his disciples, who knew and felt this Spirit in themselves, wished to practice the vengeance of Elijah, he reminded them of the difference between Elijah's spirit and his own and said to them (Luke 9 [:55-56]):[27] "You do not know what spirit you are of, for the Son of Man has not come to destroy the lives of human beings but to save them." Therefore his own, also, may never destroy anyone. Did this accusing, vengeful Elijah also have the Spirit of Christ (2 Kings 1 [:10])? If so, according to these prophets, Christ was wrong to forbid his disciples to exercise vengeance when they appealed to Elijah. (It is important to distinguish between the Spirit of God and of Christ in their functions in the different bodily and spiritual commissions given by God.)[28]

Again, self-seeking decks itself out with the love of the neighbour and says: "Should I not aid my neighbour as I am obligated and am able when someone tries to destroy him? God commanded me not to abandon my neighbour when I see him in trouble, for should I not do as I expect to be done by (Matt. 7 [:12])?" Peter wanted to give such bodily help to the Lord Christ. But note what Christ did to him whom Peter, because of his natural love for Christ, attacked and injured. The Lord restored his body to health (Luke 22 [:51]). The Lord did not desire then, nor does he today, any help through which someone else is injured or hated. We are to love our greatest enemies and not hate them (Luke 6 [:27]), even though they assault us together or singly. There is one head and one body under Christ the head, and no separate members. If one member suffers, the other is obligated [Biiiv] to suffer with it (1 Cor. 12 [:26]). It is the body of patience and love. We may not injure anyone for love of someone else or we revoke our love for the enemy and so miss the way of Christ. We would simply have a carnal agreement such as is common in the world: if you help me, I will help you. However, coming to the aid of someone in need (whether I do it or any who receive Christ in truth) regardless of whether friend or foe, so long as it can be done without hurting anyone else, will not cease or be found wanting among true Christians. For the true love of Christ their master, and through his own words which were demonstrated by him in his love for his enemies even into death, they too will witness to their enemies even in death. Such is the true wholesome love of Christ which injures no one, neither friend nor foe. Christ has this spiritual covenant with his own by means of a free, willing spirit which Christ mediated from the Father to those who have faith in him. [He accomplished this][29] through the obedience of the Spirit. It was not available to and could not be done by flesh and blood or its agencies, nor by the coercion of governments or subjects. For even with Christ himself (Matt. 16 [26:41]), the flesh was weak but the Spirit was willing and obedient. Wherever carnal government intrudes into the kingdom of Christ, Christ has died in vain in obedience to the Father. He showed and demonstrated this obedience, which is only patience and love, in cross and tribulation towards friends and foes, but exercised no other dominion, coercion, or rule, however much our opponents try to prove it by Scripture, using it as they do for their own self-justification, Whoever will be the greatest should be the servant of all (Matt. 20 [:26]). [Wherever temporal and spiritual power are conferred] there will be only a carnal glory.[30]

Those who contradict us accuse Christ and his own of opposing the Emperor and forbidding payment of taxes, refusing him obedience, saying government is not necessary, wanting to be our own lords, and appointing ourselves a king of the Jews and the like.[31] Observe the cunning and the tricks which Satan and his own employ. Out of the surfeit of their own wickedness they accuse Christ and his own of that which they themselves do. [Bivr].

A question: Suppose someone from the world or the so-called Christians, old or new,[32] who wishes to justify the use of the temporal sword with an appeal to Christ, achieves power, don't you suppose the whole lot would want to rule, and quarrel over who was to rule over them? Unless, of course, every individual would want to rule himself, so that no one else could exercise temporal rule over him because of his self-centredness. These people demand only protection and security.[33] However, no one wants to endure the authority that goes with the protection, for Authority may deal justly or unjustly according to the destiny set by God, who determines the punishment that will be meted out. Thus Pilate, by his authority received from above, judged the innocent Christ (John 19 [:11]), and Christ endured it. Nor did Christ demand the protection from Pilate which Pilate was obligated to give as part of his authority. Christ did not demand nor desire it, for the lambs of God must be ruled over with violence until the end of the world. For this reason also Peter and Paul (Rom. 13 [:l], 1 Pet. 2 [:13]), counsel submission to all human temporal Authority, ready even to die under it. Both of them indicate the limits of that obedience. Christians will not rule or dominate anyone with force. Rather they suffer violence in obedience to God and to the praise of their leader Christ. To the question raised above the lambs now reply: Who are more obedient to government, those who want to be protected and not suffer any authority, or those who desire no protection and endure all violence in the love of God? O blind and perverted nature! You are reduced to silence in this judgement.

But this perverted lot do as they always do. They boast and claim for themselves the rule of Christ and his Spirit, but in fact crave for an authority other than that of Christ's spirit. They come appealing to Christ, but they want a king only to give them security and not to have authority over them. They want to do as the heathen do. Listen to what Samuel told the Jews (1 Sam. 8 [:11]) when they demanded a protector like the heathen had. He told them that such a king would also exercise authority over them as was his right. [Bivv]. God said to Samuel that the people had not rejected Samuel but God himself and granted them the request that was their downfall. In a similar vein Christ said to his disciples: "You do not know what you are asking" (Matt. 20 [:22]). Then he offered them the chalice of his patient suffering. This is the sovereignty with which the Son of Man rules and reigns with his own through the Spirit.

In another place Jesus said to his disciples: "You know that among the Gentiles those who want to be regarded as rulers lord it over them, and the powerful are tyrants over them. But it is not so among you; rather, whoever wishes to become great among you must be your servant, and whoever wishes to be first among you must be servant of all" (Mark 10 [:42-44]). Whoever will not be admonished and disciplined in the education and correction of the Spirit is no Christian (Heb. 12 [:8]); he will be subject to the law (Gal. 3). The Word of the Lord is the only judge and sword of Christians (Eph. 6 [:17], Matt. 10 [:19-20]). True Christians will use no other judge nor sword, and whoever rejects this rejects not Christ but the Father who sent him (Matt. 10 [:32-33]). Remember that it was not Samuel who was rejected but God, and here we have much more than Samuel, Moses, patriarchs, and prophets (Matt. 12 [:42]). They are rejecting the Son and not the servant [Mark 12:32-33]. If they have treated the servants with such disrespect, how much more will they do it to the Son? The so-called Christians get their due according to their desires when God gives them rulers aplenty who will administer the king's justice. For according to the words of Christ, they demanded rulers such as the heathen have, and these will zealously impose their rule with violence. Christ reduced the heathen and Jewish law into a single law. According to Eph. 2 [:14] he broke down the middle wall of partition and put all heathen and Jewish laws together. For both Jewish and Gentile laws govern carnal man. But they do not govern the spiritual Christ, for whoever does not have the spirit of Christ does not belong to him (Rom. 8 [:91]). Those who are liberated from these laws become subject to Christ. It is a new birth from flesh and death to spirit and life (1 John 3, 4, 5). [Cir] This spiritual life is nothing but love and patience; neither Moses nor heathen but only Christians will be found there. Outside of Christ neither the law of the Jews nor of the heathen (who are their own law according to Rom. 2 [:141) promote life; they are simply a bridle for the wickedness of carnal ignorance. No matter how upright the flesh may be without the Spirit it has to be bridled. We know that some animals are more compliant than others – the difference, for example, between horses and donkeys. Still, they all need to be bridled (Ps. 32 [:9]). This bridle is not Christ but the dead letter of the law and human commandments (Gal. 3 [:23-25]). For quite outside the fear of the law, the Spirit of Christ gives life. "For all who are led by the Spirit of God are the children of God. For you did not receive a spirit of slavery to fall back into fear but you have received a spirit of adoption through which we cry, 'Abba, pater.' Thus we are children and heirs if, in fact, we suffer with him" (Rom. 8 [:14-17]). Notice that he does not say "rule with him." Neither Christ nor his own ever reprove anyone on the basis of the law either Jewish or heathen, but only through the Word of the Father which is Christ. Whoever does not have Christ also does not live according to the Word, and there is nothing but flesh without spirit. Those who have Christ have the Word as a reliable ruler in the heart and no other is necessary, as Paul says in Col. 1 [:27-28]. Those who reprove by means other than the Word, which is Christ (John 1 [:1-2], 8 [:32-42]), are rulers of darkness. He admonished those who had entered the kingdom of the Word [Col. 1:12-13] which is the Son, the light of the world, who enlightens all people (John 1 [:9]) to be grateful.

From now on, for those who are outside of Christ the laws of the Jews and of the heathen are a single reality. In Christ there is neither Jew nor Greek but one living creation in God (Gal. 3 [:28], 5 [:6], 6 [:15]). Regardless of this, the so-called evangelical Christians reject imperial law under the appearance of godliness to disguise their fleshly ambition and for the securing of their property, position, and reputation.[34] They judge according to the law of Moses and pollute the Lord Jesus Christ with blood.[35] Outside of Christ the laws of Jews and Gentiles are one single [Civ] law. Thus, no matter how much they oppose the law of the Emperor, their false pretension will not help them, for Christ is the end of the law for the justification of everyone who has faith (Rom. 10 [:4]). Similarly, Paul writes the Corinthians (1 Cor. 6 [:1-8]) that they have failed Christ because they demanded temporal rights, and that from unbelievers. Is there no wisdom of Christ among you, Paul continues, by which one could admonish the other in patience and love? And even if the least of all the members of the church [Eph. 3:8], urges you to the patience and love of Christ (if indeed you were brethren of love and peace) and to judge your own cases, you still insist on doing it before unbelievers. For the brotherhood of Christ is patience and love, does not have nor desires to have either Authority or subjects, but is one in Christ. For where there is no Authority there can also be no subject.

Still, the true Christians are subject to all creatures for the sake of God and Christ.[36] He has come who was to precede Christ, and at that time the life of the flesh had to be sustained through the fear of the law without the living power of Christ and his Spirit until the time of Christ (Gal. 3 [:24]). Until then the sceptre and the dominion remained with the tribe of Judah from whom Christ was descended after the flesh (Rom. 1 [:3], 9 [:53], Rev. 5 [:5], Heb. 7 [:14]). That is the meaning of the words of the patriarch Jacob to his son Judah (Gen. 49 [:10]): "Neither the sceptre nor the ruler's staff from between his feet shall depart from his seed until the appointed one comes[37] to whom the people will give their obedience." These words of Jacob also imply that at the coming of Christ the sceptre would be taken away from the fleshly people of God and they would be thrown out among the Gentiles to be the swineherds of the empire. For all earthly sovereignties and imperiums are only the destructive work of wild boars before God's countenance, because they destroy the vineyard of God (Ps. 80 [:7-13]). All the sovereigns, protectors, and rulers are only swineherds in contrast to the sovereignty of Christ which now rules in his own, for outside of Christ there is absolutely no faith regardless of whether one be Jew, Gentile, or so-called Christian (John 15 [:5], 2 John 1, 3, John 1 [:17]). He who does not submit to be admonished and disciplined through the fear of the word of Christ is no Christian. [Ciir] Whoever seeks to admonish and discipline by means other than the gentle and humble word of Christ (which alone is patience and love), such as with the law of God through the letter and the external sword, as the so-called Christians do, that one too is no Christian. To Christ has been given authority over all flesh (Matt. 28 [:18]) in order that he may bring that flesh into complete fear and discipline through his Spirit (Rom. 8 [:9-11]). Christ does not kill but bring to life (John 6 [:40], 2 Cor. 3 [:6]), and no one may take the sword of Moses, the man of God, because Moses himself surrendered it at his departure and, pointing to Christ, said: A man will arise from among your brothers; listen to him (Deut. 18 [:15]). Christ himself witnessed and said: "If you believed Moses, you would believe in me, for he wrote about me" (John 5 [:46]). Salvation comes from the Jews (John 4 [:22]). Since Christ came Moses is no longer authoritative, for he had only the sword of the law but not of the Spirit. To Christ we must listen, through the Word, which is a double-edged sword to distinguish good from evil (Heb. 4 [:12]). This evil belongs to the sword of the wicked and wicked rulers who, expressing their own carnal mentality, preserve carnal peace with each other for the sake of property and position. Christ cannot be reconciled with Belial (2 Cor. 6 [:15]). The peace of Christ is different. It brings unrest without any injury to whomever possesses it because of the flesh and [what remains] of self-centredness, and peace to friends and foes. This is the peace of Christ about which Christ says that he gives it not as the world gives, for the world treasures peace only for the securing of property and position. If it is injured in any way, there is nothing but turmoil.

The early Christians to the time of Constantine exercised no temporal rule or sword among themselves. The command of their master did not allow it. He granted them only the sword of the Word. Whoever, after sufficient admonition would not listen, was regarded as a Gentile [Ciiv] and unbeliever [Matt. 18:17]. But when at that time, the pope, as a servant of the church was married to Leviathan,[38] that is, temporal power, but in the disguise of Christ, the Antichrist was conceived and born as has now been revealed. The mystery of iniquity was long concealed (2 Thess. 2 [:3ff.]). For a very long time she fortified herself with Scripture under a guise of godliness until the wickedness of the apparently holy clergy was exposed, which is also now the case with the new Antichrist.[39] They are false shepherds to whom the sheep do not belong; they enter through the roof and come only to devour, plunder, and kill (John 10 [:10]). The spiritual devil and his multitude, a murderer from the beginning (John 8 [:44]), entered the sheepfold with violence and stole and wrested the sword from the secular Authority. No heathen tyrant ever murdered and killed so thoroughly. The most horrible monster, turning even against its own kind, tramples, crushes, and ravages with its feet what it does not eat and devastates it with the counterfeit ban [Eze. 34:17-19]. Thus the abominable wickedness reveals itself. Some true sons of Pilate still ask whether Christ is a king. When, in the attempt to save Jesus from the false Jews, that is, from those who falsely confess faith in God, and who even today still hand Jesus over [to the executioner], they are told in Christ's words that his kingdom is not of this world (John 18 [:36]), they say that they want no king whose kingdom is not of this world but an emperor whose kingdom is of this world. They are consistent: since they are children of this world and not of God, they must needs be ruled by those cosmic authorities who fight against Christ (Eph. 6 [:12]). They don't want to be ruled by Christ for he is, in their view, a preposterous king. When the people wanted to make a temporal king of Jesus to ensure the temporal food they had received from him, he left them and fled (John 6 [:15]). Everyone should completely depart from these prophets who betroth the patient, loving Christ to the secular Authority under the pretence that it is spiritual, to ensure that a new [Ciiir] Antichrist is born or fashioned. I hope that the Lord will prevent his own from becoming wild boars and swineherds who destroy the vineyard (Ps. 79 [:1], 80 [:13]), but will instead be preserved as sheep and shepherds who tend the vineyard, do not graze it bare, and that Christ remains our arch-shepherd now and forever. Amen.

Lastly and to conclude, I remind all who mix the kingdom of Christ with the secular Authority, and who now propose to judge between the good and the evil or wish to pull up [the weeds] by means other than the Spirit of God, of the parable and judgement of Christ (Matt. 13 [:24-30]): "The kingdom of heaven may be compared to a man who sowed good seed in his field; but when everybody was asleep, an enemy came and sowed weeds among the wheat, and then went away. So when the plants came up and bore grain, then the weeds appeared as well. Then the servants of the householder came and said to him, 'Master, did you not sow good seed in your field? Where, then, did these weeds come from?' He answered, 'An enemy has done this.' The servants said to him, 'Then do you want us to go and pull out the weeds?' But he replied, 'No, certainly not; for in gathering the weeds you would uproot the wheat along with them. Let both of them grow together until the harvest, and at harvest time I will tell the reapers, 'Collect the weeds first and bind them in bundles to be burned, but gather the wheat into my barn.'"[40]

Listen to Christ's interpretation of the parable when the disciples asked him about its meaning, and let these nay-sayers themselves judge whether Christ committed the sword of secular Authority to his own, or whether he commanded them to gather in the weeds before the End of the world. Jesus answered his disciples: "The one who sows the good seed is the Son of Man; the field is the world, and the good seed are the children of the kingdom; the weeds are the children of the evil one, and the enemy who sowed them [Ciiiv] is the devil; the harvest is the end of the age, and the reapers are the angels. Just as the weeds are collected and burned up with fire, so will it be at the end of the age. The Son of Man will send his angels, and they will collect out of his kingdom all causes of sin and all evil-doers, and they will throw them into the furnace of fire where there will be weeping and gnashing of teeth. Then the righteous will shine like the sun in the kingdom of their Father. Let anyone with ears listen!" [Matt. 13:37-43].

Our opponents should take note of what the Lord Christ says to his servants to whom it is given only to judge that which is external and at the present time but never that which is internal and eternal. For he is the saviour for everyone's salvation and not their destroyer (up to the time of the final irreversible judgement after which the time for repentance is over). Christ told this parable only to ensure that the grace of God would not be cut off for human beings and that the wheat would not be pulled out with the weeds. For as long as a person remains in this mortal life, no matter how wicked he may be, he may be converted to a better life through the grace of Christ and the patience and love shown to him by those around him. For there are twelve hours in the day as the Lord himself said (John 11 [:9]) [during which a man may be converted], but if he is pulled up like a weed, he can never repent. For this reason Christ, who is patient and humble, commands his disciples (John 13 [:12-15], Matt. 11 [:29]) to learn from him and to wait faithfully for the erring one during the time of his life. He also instructs his own by the foregoing parable to wait. He commands no one to condemn and kill with the sword. Virtually the whole of Matt. chapter 5 testifies that no one is to be coerced or dominated. Rather, the disciples allow themselves to be forced and dominated and to submit to what is done to them with patience. Those who do the opposite are of the world and are not Christ's, are unbelievers and do not have faith. Those who fight with the sword will be condemned by the sword (Rev. 13 [:10], Matt. 16 [:25]). [Civr] Hence all those who came into the world since Christ, who is the sharp sword of the Word, and have not believed will destroy and devour each other with the sword (Luke 21 [:24]).[41] Whoever does not believe is condemned already (John 3 [:18]). Further, the Lord said to those who wanted to follow him that they should let the dead bury their dead (Matt. 8 [:22]). There is no godliness outside of Christ. The 'godliness' of the flesh and of evildoers is nothing but wickedness and uncleanness.[42] In Christ, through faith, the only sword is the Word; with this only Christians judge and are judged. They have not been commanded by Christ to use any other sword. Christians should avoid and separate themselves from all who don't believe this, until they are converted. Those who come to believe it should be received in patience and love. This is the true judgement of Christians in this time, and Christ has neither committed to them nor commanded them any other judgement.

The true Christians will use this purity in the liberty of the Spirit in which they remain pure and in which all things are pure for them [Luke 11:41; John 13:10-11]. Nothing is pure outside that which serves love in the hopeful confidence of faith and is expressed in gentleness, patience, and humility, regardless of how fervently Satan preens himself with Paul's words in Titus 1 [:15]: "To the pure all things are pure, but to the corrupt and unbelieving nothing is pure." Whatever Christ has named or commanded is what comprises "all things" in Christ. These are faith, love, hope, patience, gentleness, humility, purity of heart, thoughtfulness. These and all other virtues and knowledge are pure only through faith, which is purity itself. Outside of faith all virtues and knowledge, regardless of how prized they may be, are in and of themselves impure and an abomination before the face of God. Many upright heathen are known to us.[43] They indeed had great discipline, virtue, and knowledge, but to them it was all impure before the face of God because of their unbelief. Everything would be impure if one did not have faith in Christ, even if one did the works of angels, apostles, even of Christ himself. [Civv] It is thus that Paul came to the view that all virtues outside of faith in Christ are impure and all of them are pure because of faith. [But] Paul's words may never be taken to mean that one may take anything outside of what Christ commanded and employ it and preen oneself with the liberty of Christ, as Satan does. True Christians will never take the liberty to exercise coercion and Authority, regardless of how wicked or upright those to be ruled might be. Rather they will allow themselves to be dominated, ruled over, and violated in patience and love to the end of time. Let us continue to be servants as our Master and Christ served and allowed himself to be ruled over and violated. Christ came not to be served, not to rule in the world according to the flesh.

We don't need to be concerned about governmental Authority. There will always be those who want to rule. Let us see to it that we remain Christians, live patiently, and accept the victory of the Lamb to the glory of our Father and of his Christ. To him alone belongs all the glory, power, majesty, praise and honour now and to eternity. Amen.

[*Note 1*][44]
I am surprised that Christ and the apostles, and especially Saint Peter, did not elect a ruler to rule over all those whom he converted to Christ and who believed, as we read in Acts chapter 2. The Spirit of God was not wise enough at that time for these prophets who are rightly called the "new" evangelicals. God have mercy on them. Why did God not allow the tribe of Levi a portion of the promised land nor any external authority to rule (Deut. 18 [:1-2], Josh. 14 [:3])? How much less would he give it to the spiritual and royal priests of Christ so ordained, forever under the order of Melchisedek, and under which all flesh and all its authorities must come to nothing. (What the figurative meaning of this priesthood in Christ and attributed to us is, can be learned from Paul in Hebrews, [Dir] chapters 7, 8, 9, and 10.) Christ himself says in Luke 9 [:58] that the Son of Man has no place where he can lay his head.

[*Note 2*]
The first council of the Holy Spirit was established by the Apostles. Its decision was written and carried to Antioch by Judas and Silas, who also [delivered it] verbally. It pleased the Holy Spirit and the Apostles not to lay any legal burdens on the churches except for the three most necessary provisions. These were that they abstain from what was offered to idols, from blood, from what is strangled, and from fornication. If they kept these, all would be well (Acts 15 [:22-29]). This text, read and understood literally, would only be more Jewish legalism rather than liberty, were it not that a particular mystery is hidden under the words and kept concealed until our time.[45] In fact it was the Spirit of God speaking through the Apostles concerning the future time which would come. It has all now been revealed; the sacrifice to idols of the pope and the Antichrist is far more idolatrous and abominable before the face of God than all the idol sacrifices of the heathen. For Paul says in 1 Cor. 10 [:27] that if he were not told that it was offered to idols, he would eat it. However, if he were told that it had been offered to idols, he would not eat. Thus the pope's idolatry is not simply a sacrifice to idols but the idol itself. The Antichrist and those who run with him are now urging all of us to eat. That is why the Spirit of God calls it a necessary thing and something to be avoided.

Second, concerning blood and what was strangled, the Holy Spirit did not mean to repeat the law of Moses, but rather referred to the words in Ps. 16 [:4]: "their drink-offerings of blood I will not pour out." This, too, has been revealed in this last time. At the point at which the temporal power mixed itself into the kingdom of Christ,[46] as shown above, the eating of blood by those who pretended to be Christians began as they killed people. Today the Holy Spirit forbids this and warns us to refrain from what is strangled. [Div] It is the source of all shedding of blood, namely the self-serving, wealth, and glory of the world. The Lord Christ also refers to what is strangled in Matt. 13 [:7]. It is the seed that fell among thorns, and the thorns grew up and choked it and it bore no fruit. This strangled word is completely in the power of the Antichrist's kingdom and virtually all people eat of it, ignoring the faithful warning of the Holy Spirit. May God preserve his own.

Third, the fornication mentioned is not only the physical
fornication which is the fruit of spiritual fornication, but
of that whore with whom all the kings of the earth and
all the people with them have fornicated and still do
as is evident. It is needful that as the children
of God we should prepare and protect
ourselves against all this.
If we do it we do
right. Farewell
in the com-
fort of the
Spirit.
Amen

# Notes

[1] This translation is based on a photocopy of the original which appeared in the *Mennonite Quarterly Review* 32 (1958), 34-47, as part of the article "An Early Anabaptist Treatise on the Christian and the State" by Hans J. Hillerbrand. The original title is: *Aufdeckung der Babylonischen Hurn/ vnd Antichrists alten vnnd newen gehaimnusz vnnd grewel/ Auch vom sig/ frid vn herrschung warhaffter Christen/ vn wie sy der Oberkait gehorsamen/ das creutz on aufruhr vnd gegenweer/ mit Christo inn gedult vnd liebe tragen/ zum preisz Gottes/ vnd allen frumen vnd Gottsuchenden zu dienst/ stercke vnd besserung/ an tag gebracht.*

[2] The rule to which Marpeck refers here is the sharing of believers in the rule and sovereignty of Christ, which is not physical and earthly but spiritual and heavenly. It is a contrast he is at great pains to emphasize throughout this tract.

[3] The biblical quotations are both from Luther's translation, which Marpeck uses throughout the tract.

[4] This adjective (*sodomitisch*) is a reference to the ungodly behaviour of the citizens of Sodom described in Gen. 18-19.

[5] The reference here is to the mystery of the whore in Rev. 17:5-7.

[6] The identification of the Great Whore with Rome and the papacy was made in the Middle Ages by, among others, Joachim of Fiore, Petrarch, and the Waldensians. See Bernard McGinn, *Visions of the End: Apocalyptic Traditions in the Middle Ages* (New York: Columbia University Press, 1979), 163, 244, and 219 respectively. See also Dante in *The Divine Comedy*, Inferno, Canto XIX. Martin Luther made the same identification in, for example, his German Bible of 1534 in the engraving by the anonymous Meister MS illustrating Rev. 17, and in the marginal gloss which reads: "Hie zeiget er die Roemische kirche/ jnn jrer gestalt vn wesen/ die verdampt sol werden." The engraving shows the Whore wearing the papal triple tiara.

[7] Marpeck clearly means the Anabaptist *Gemeinden.*

[8] Marpeck here conflates the images of the Great Whore and the Red Dragon. This is because both of these images, drawn from Rev. 17 and 13, are symbols of the last great rebellion against God.

[9] There were long and unresolved controversies about baptism and the Lord's Supper, chiefly between Lutherans and Zwinglians. See Luther's "Pagan Servitude of the Church," in *Martin Luther: Selections from His Writings,* ed. John Dillenberger (New York: Doubleday, 1961), 255-59. In 1529, shortly before Marpeck wrote this tract, Luther and Zwingli, Philip Melanchthon, and Johannes Oecolampadius had a debate at Marburg specifically on the Lord's Supper. See *Great Debates of the Reformation,* ed. Donald J. Ziegler (New York: Random House, 1969), 71-107, for a record of those talks.

[10] This is a reflection of Luther's view of the real presence of Christ in the sacrament.

[11] One of the consequences of the politicization of the Reformation was the gradual development of a military league for the defence of the evangelical faith against the growing threat of military action by the Emperor Charles V and the Catholic Princes. The Schmalcaldic League, concluded in February 1530, was the result. The main members of

the League were John of Saxony, Philip of Hesse, and the cities of Magdeburg, Strasbourg, Ulm, and Constance.

[12] The Lamb here (Rev. 13:8) is both Jesus and those who follow him. As Jesus was crucified, so they are martyred. They are not two but one.

[13] Marpeck's original word is *Gewalt*, a synonym for the word *Obrigkeit*, which Luther used in his translation of Rom. 13:1, where it means governing authorities. Marpeck appears to avoid this word deliberately and seems to be working with the text of Rom. 13 from the Zurich Froschauer Bible, which uses *oberkeit* and *gwalt*. I have chosen to use the word "Authority" in the translation because it conveys what Marpeck is saying better than "power," which is a more literal translation. Wherever "Authority" appears in upper case in this translation, it means governmental authority.

[14] So the Lutherans referred to themselves because they claimed to have recovered the true Gospel. Marpeck evidently has some doubts about their right to use the term.

[15] Marpeck's argument was specifically with the Lutherans with whom he had much in common.

[16] The Lutheran theologians.

[17] In his work "Against the Robbing and Murdering Hordes of Peasants" (1525), Luther wrote: "Anyone who is killed fighting on the side of the rulers may be a true martyr in the eyes of God, if he fights with the kind of conscience I have just described . . . . These are strange times, when a prince can win heaven with bloodshed better than other men with prayer!" *Selected Writings of Martin Luther 1523-1526*, ed. T. G. Tappert (Philadelphia: Fortress Press, 1967), 353, 354.

[18] Marpeck refers here to the freedom from all external observances which were required of the faithful in the late medieval church.

[19] Marpeck's characteristic word here is *aigenthumb* and further on, *vnser aigenthumb*. It means not simply property as in modern German usage, but rather what is *eigen*, peculiar or characteristic of the unregenerate person.

[20] See the foregoing note.

[21] This is an incomplete sentence beginning "Vnd wiewol wir sehe das die zwen man von Christo (die grosz schade than haben/ vn von in noch heuet niemant in der welt sicher ist) erledigt sein/ vn nun Christo nachfolgen." The translation is therefore, in part, a conjecture.

[22] Marpeck uses *Gergisaner* following Luther and Zwingli. The more reliable manuscripts read *Gadarenon*, rendered *Gadarener* in the revised Luther translation, and *Gadarenes* in the New Revised Standard Version.

[23] See Martin Luther in "Temporal Authority: To What Extent it Should be Obeyed" in Tappert, 281.

[24] Marpeck's words are: *vnderm schein Christi*.

[25] Marpeck's words are: *geschlecht des aigenthumbs*.

[26] Marpeck means here especially the distinctions to be made between Old and New Testaments, and especially the distinction between promise and fulfilment.

[27] This quotation from Luke 9:56 is not found in recent translations because it lacks convincing manuscript evidence.

[28] The *Testamentserleüterung*, a work of Marpeck and his co-workers done sometime in the 1540s, deals specifically with the careful distinctions to be made between Old and New Testaments as they are used by Christians. This does not imply devaluing the Old Testament as is sometimes claimed. They saw a historical development from the one to the other, and understood the appearance of Christ to be the fulfilment of what had been anticipated in Old Testament times. See William Klassen, *Covenant and Community: The Life, Writings and Hermeneutics of Pilgram Marpeck* (Grand Rapids: Eerdmans, 1967), 51-53, 108-130.

[29] A verb is missing in this sentence or else the punctuation is misleading.

[30] Marpeck's words are: *Da wirt ain schlechte leibliche herrligkait verhanden sein.*

[31] This could be a reference to the claims made by Augustin Bader for his infant son in 1528. Bader had called a meeting of Anabaptists near Strasbourg to convince them of his views regarding the endtime. Marpeck would certainly have known about that event, after which Bader announced that his little son was to be king in anticipation of the reign of Christ. See Werner O. Packull, *Mysticism and the Early South German-Austrian Anabaptist Movement 1525-1531* (Scottdale: Herald Press, 1977), 130-38.

[32] "Old or new" means "Papal or Protestant."

[33] The whole passage beginning with "A question" reads as follows: *Ain frag/vnd tret ainer ausz der welt kindern/ vnd allen vermainten Christen/ newe vn alt (so das leiblich schwert im schein Christi erhalten woellen) auf die ban/ ob sy nit mit jrem hauffen begeren/ vnd zancken darub/ leiblich zuherrschen/ vn wolt Got/ das nit ain yeder fuer sich selbs beger zuherrschen/ damit das niemant leiblicher weisz ueber jn Herr sey/ um seiner aigennuetzigkait willen/ vnd begerb nur den schutz/ schirm vn sicherhait.*

[34] Again Marpeck's word is *aigenthumb*. Here it clearly means physical property but also position and reputation, everything on which they depend for their self-esteem.

[35] This is Marpeck's reference to the use of the Old Testament by the Reformers to justify resort to arms.

[36] This passage is a clear echo of Luther's words in his 1520 tract *The Freedom of a Christian*: "A Christian is a perfectly free lord of all, subject to none. A Christian is a perfectly dutiful servant of all, subject to all." Tappert, 20.

[37] Luther's rendering of this is: *Bisz dass der Held komme*, "Until the champion comes."

[38] This appears to be the only known reference to the state or secular power as Leviathan before its use by Thomas Hobbes in his famous work by that name.

[39] A reference to the already developing Protestant clericalism.

[40] The translation is, on the whole, that of the New Revised Standard Version with minor modifications reflecting Marpeck's rendering.

[41] This reference indicates that Marpeck believed himself to be living near the End.

[42] The original of this reads: *dan kain frummkait ist ausser Christo/ so sein uebel thaeter vnnd flaisch frumm/ als boszhait vnd vnrain.*

[43] Among the upright heathen people, the first to be thought of was Cornelius, the Roman centurion in Acts 10, and the Roman centurion in Luke 7. Likewise Plato and Aristotle and other Greek and Roman philosophers were often regarded as upright.

[44] Notes 1 and 2 are so designated because it appears that Marpeck added these reflections after he had completed the tract. Both notes add further support for his main thesis, which is that no coercion or domination of others, including that inflicted by governments, can ever be justified by appeal to Christ.

[45] The following interpretation is an example of pre-Reformation exegetical method, a level of spiritual interpretation relating particularly to the church.

[46] While a little awkward, this is an accurate rendition of the words: *so bald der leiblich gewalt . . . sich in das reich Christi vermischet hat.* The active voice rather than the passive is used here, which indicates Marpeck's view that the kingdom of Christ was invaded by the secular power with the intention of destroying it.

# A New Dialogue
[Anonymous]

Translated
with an introduction
by
**Werner O. Packull**

# Introduction

In his book, *The Inner Word and the Outer World*, Patrick Hayden-Roy drew attention to an Anabaptist pamphlet currently in the City Archive of Ulm.[1] The pamphlet, bound into a collective volume [Sammelband] of archival documents,[2] carries the title *A New Dialogue/ Question and Answers between a Preacher and a Baptist/ Concerning Preaching/ the Eucharist/ Baptism and Proper Christian Community/ Delightful to Read*[3] (hereafter *New Dialogue*). Hayden-Roy gave a brief description of the pamphlet's content and suggested that it had been imported from Augsburg to Ulm by a certain Matheus Strizell (Sturizell).[4] My findings confirm the Augsburg origin of the pamphlet and that it was composed in 1531 or 1532, although neither author, printer, date nor place of publication is given.[5] The date of composition can be established with some certainty because of a reference to Martin Luther's "German Mass and Order of Service,"[6] which the author claims to have read five or six years earlier. Since Luther's work appeared in 1526, the *New Dialogue* was composed in 1531 or 1532, which fits the time frame established by Hayden-Roy.

My further investigation revealed that the *New Dialogue* existed in another edition, that is, as Part Two of a pamphlet entitled *A Beautiful Dialogue between a Noble and his Servant Concerning Apostolic Baptism and Obedience to Authority* (hereafter *Beautiful Dialogue*).[7] The *Beautiful Dialogue* had been examined long ago by Karl Schottenloher. On the basis of the allusion to Luther's "German Mass" found in Part Two, he had dated the *Beautiful Dialogue* as coming from Philip Ulhart's press in 1532.[8] But Schottenloher was unaware that Part Two existed as a separate, independent edition in Ulm's Archive under a different title with different dialogue partners. In the *New Dialogue* the partners are a Preacher [Predikant] and a Baptist [Täufer]; in Part Two of the *Beautiful Dialogue* the partners are a Pastor [Pfarherr] and the Servant of a noble. The actual conversation in the *New Dialogue* corresponds verbatim with that in Part Two of the *Beautiful Dialogue*. Part Two carries the title *How the Pastor Sends for the Servant. And How They Converse Further with Each Other Concerning the Office of Preaching, Baptism, Lord's Supper and Proper Christian Congregation*.[9]

I discovered further that Schottenloher's dating of the *Beautiful Dialogue* and its Part Two had been mistaken. Two years before Hayden-Roy gave notice of his discovery in Ulm, scholars of the former GDR rejected Schottenloher's dating of the *Beautiful Dialogue*, and on the basis of print history and lettering revised the date to the mid 1540s – Ulhart's "late period." But the internal evidence found in Part Two led them to speculate that the *Beautiful Dialogue* must have circulated in manuscript form from 1532 until its printing in the mid 1540s.[10] That scenario too has to be revised, because we now have irrefutable evidence that as early as 1532 Part Two of the *Beautiful Dialogue* existed as an independent print under the title *New Dialogue*. Whether Part One existed as a separate print prior to 1545 remains unknown, because so far no such print has surfaced.

Before we turn to the significance of the second edition, a brief investigation of the circumstances surrounding the appearance of the *New Dialogue* in 1532 is called for. After a period of dormancy, Anabaptist activity revived in Augsburg during the early 1530s. On Sunday, March 5, 1531 two Anabaptist missionaries, Hans Kentner and Jos Riemer, took the pulpit at St. Ulrich in order to publicize the Anabaptist cause.[11] Kentner had been baptized by Philip Plener,[12] who in the fall of 1528 had decided for a moratorium on baptism in Augsburg's territory because the response to the Anabaptist message had been ephemeral. Kentner had apparently resumed where Philip left off and established a small conventicle of Anabaptists in Täferdingen, near Augsburg. Philip, meanwhile, had gathered a contingent of followers and settled in Moravia.

By March 1531 Kentner must have considered the situation in Augsburg opportune for a public statement. The authorities were not amused. They arrested Kentner, Riemer, and their supporters. City reformers were ordered to instruct the prisoners, a task assigned to two recent arrivals from Strasbourg, Wolfgang Musculus, pastor [Pfarrer] at the Church of the Holy Cross, and Bonifacius Wolfhart, preacher [Predikant] at St. Ann.[13] Musculus was a former Benedictine, who had served as Martin Bucer's secretary and Matthias Zell's assistant. He came to represent a Bucerian Reformed position in Augsburg, while his colleague Wolfhart proved to be a Zwinglian with Schwenckfeldian sympathies. Wolfhart's inaugural sermons on the sacraments so emphasized their spiritual, inner meaning that "many Anabaptists" allegedly "reconciled with the Augsburg church."[14] Not surprisingly, more conservative Lutherans considered Wolfhart a proto-Anabaptist or Schwenckfeldian.

Given these circumstances, the incident of March 5, 1531 takes on a more realistic hue. The Anabaptists, led by Kentner and Riemer, must have hoped for improved relations with the city's reformers. During interrogations they explained that their actions were motivated by "love of

God and neighbour." They no longer wanted to spread their ideas secretly. With the evangelical party in ascendancy they hoped for tolerance and dialogue. However, these expectations proved unrealistic, although the prison conversations with Musculus and Wolfhart did lead to an agreement of sorts. Kentner and a number of his fellow prisoners gained release through recantation. But Kentner soon regretted concessions made under duress. Both he and Riemer resumed their Anabaptist ministry.[15]

These events of 1531 provide background and context to the religious climate in which the *New Dialogue* was conceived. It is possible that Kentner and/or Riemer composed the *New Dialogue* as a cathartic-apologetic exercise. The accusation that the Preacher agreed with the Baptist in private could point to Wolfhart. He seems to fit the role of the sympathetic Predikant, who agreed that proper administration of the sacraments and church discipline was possible only in small conventicles, but who desired to remain at his post for a year or two in order to first win more citizens for the evangelical cause.

But Kentner and Riemer do not exhaust the list of potential authors. Others appeared on the scene in 1532, among them Georg Probst Rotenfelder, also known as Jörg Maler. Before his baptism in March/April 1532 Maler served as cantor at St. Andrew's in Augsburg. His baptizer, Sebold Feuchter,[16] was the son of a Nuremberg mint master and a goldsmith by trade, whose sufferings on behalf of the "Word of God" began during the Peasants' War. According to his own account, Feuchter had been expelled from Kaufbeuren during the uprising. A similar fate awaited him in Esslingen, this time because of his association with Anabaptism. Since his arrival in Augsburg in late 1531, he had baptized seven persons, including Maler, but he denied being an appointed leader. It is difficult to categorize Feuchter's Anabaptist beliefs; he distinguished himself from the Swiss who were allegedly prepared to use the sword [*wollen darein schlagen*]. He also distanced himself from those who refused to pay taxes or rents [*steuern und zins*], indicating his preparedness to honour all financial obligations due the proper authority. As Heinold Fast has shown, Feuchter's convert, Maler, seems equally difficult to classify.[17] Arrested within a year of his baptism, Maler's prison experience was similar to that of Kentner's. On April 29, 1533 he agreed to an ambivalent statement read to him by Wolfhart. He too came to regret his "recantation."

Whether Maler or Feuchter had a hand in drafting the *New Dialogue* remains speculation. Both belonged to the literate class of upper artisans, and Maler constitutes a historic link to the second edition of the *New Dialogue* more than a decade later. He was a member of Augsburg's Anabaptist community in 1532 when the *New Dialogue* appeared, and a member of Pilgram Marpeck's circle when the pamphlet reappeared, circa 1545, as Part Two of the *Beautiful Dialogue*. Marpeck and his circle, it is now clear, sponsored a whole series of reprints in the 1540s, including *The Exposé of the Babylonian Whore*, which first appeared in 1532, the same year as the *New Dialogue*.[18]

The translation offered here is based on the 1532 edition, or the *New Dialogue*, now in Ulm. In 1996 Dr. Specker, Director of the Stadtarchiv of Ulm, provided me with a photocopy and kindly granted permission for its translation. Thanks are also due to Ph.D. student Mrs. Mary Buck for her fine work in checking and providing the Scriptural references. These will be very useful to students of Anabaptism interested in Anabaptist biblical literacy and hermeneutics as they relate to both Testaments and the Apocrypha. The Froschauer Bible of 1531, apparently used by the author(s), may well have initiated a more wholistic approach. Our citations are from the New Revised Standard Version. In those cases where the author(s) provided a number of supporting references, we chose only to cite the first or key text.

As in the translation of the *Exposé*, folio numbers of the original document are given in square brackets in the text as, for example **[Aiir]**.

# A New Dialogue

Questions and Answers
Between a Preacher and a Baptist
Concerning Preaching, the Eucharist,
Baptism and the True Christian Community.
Delightful to Read

[Anonymous]

P[reacher]. The Preacher sends for the Baptist and says to him: Dear brother, I would like to converse with you in private and in a gracious manner, so that I may have the opportunity to ask you some questions and listen to you and you to me in a friendly and kind way.

B[aptist]. My dear friend, God commands his own that they should act graciously and wisely towards all (Phil. 4[:5]). How then could I withhold graciousness from you? But there are two kinds of friendship, just as there are two kinds of wisdom: one worldly and the other godly. They cannot be in harmony with each other. Spirit and flesh are not one (Gal. 5[:17]). He who still pleases men is not Christ's servant (Gal. 1[:10]). Flesh and blood cannot know spiritual friendship, no more than they can know divine wisdom (1 Cor. 2[:14]). Therefore, let the hypocritical friendship of the world be denied to you but not the divine, according to which I offer to listen to you with kindness and patience. And in as much as God [Aii] gives grace, I will meet with you for love's sake, to share with you in as much as is not harmful to me before God. He will reveal your heart to me.

P. I cannot reject your opinion, let it be. I will get to the heart of the matter and ask you: Why, then, do you, Baptist brethren, not come to hear my preaching nor celebrate the Lord's Supper with me and my congregation? I wish we were united with each other.

B. I am glad to answer this question. But tell me, dear friend, what is the reason that you make so many repeated inquiries of my brethren and now of me? Yet you never seem to come to any peace of mind. Something must be wrong with your heart. I fear I will not achieve much with you either.

P. Dear brother, even though not much may come of it, I do like to hear you speak about it.

B. Not the listeners but the doers are blessed (Jas. 1[:22]). It bothers my conscience to talk too much about it with you, because you only want to hear about it but not act on it. Better to be silent than to talk uselessly into the wind. It is like pouring out and wasting good wine.[19]

P. Dear brother, let those matters be for now, and give me an answer to my questions. Who knows when it is the right time? Are there not twelve hours in a day?

B. It is always the right time. God tells no one to wait for conversion until tomorrow or to postpone it from one day to the next (Eccl. 5[:4]).[20] Whoever recognizes the truth is wrong to wait. However, the proper order would have called for us to speak first about inward matters before dealing with outward things. One should first consider the inside of a cup.[21] Nevertheless, I will patiently answer concerning outward matters, with the hope that the inward will be touched upon as well. I already surmise why it is that you cannot find peace of mind. It is because your questions concern only external matters. I cannot applaud you for not wanting to hear about inner matters first. Now I will answer why we do not go to hear your sermon nor celebrate the Lord's Supper with you and members of your congregation. The reason is that you preach and teach that one should keep the will and commandments of God and Christ, but you are the first to break them.

Take, for example, child-baptism; you can neither prove it from the Scriptures nor defend it with [a good] conscience. Yet you and your kind continue to defend the practice with silly, unfounded, dishonest, dark, twisted, ridiculous Scriptural references, arguments and counter-arguments against the transparent testimonies of the Scriptures. But it will not help you, because the longer [you do so] the more your folly will be revealed to everyone (1 Tim. 3[:9]),[22] and what is not commanded or planted by the Father will be weeded out Matt. 15[:13]. It is also against the command of Christ, the apostolic order and [Aiii] custom, according to which the teaching comes first, after that believing and third baptism of adults who understand the teaching and can confess the faith. Baptism was not commanded for immature children; read Matt. 28[:19-29]; Mark 16[:15-16]; Acts 2[:38-42]; 8[:12, 35-38]; 9[:17-19]; 10[:44-48]; 17[:3-4, 11, 12]; 19[:1-5]; 22[:14-16]. Against such testimony of the New Testament all your arguments are like snowballs [directed] against a solid wall or an open square. You will never maintain child baptism against the testimony of the New Testament. Your planting will not take deep roots (Wis. 5[4:3]. But tell me one thing: If any of you, with a price on your head, were ordered to produce even one passage from the New Testament that clearly and unequivocally states in writing that Christ, Paul, or Peter baptized children or ordered them to be baptized, or a passage where the words child and baptism appear in conjunction, as is the case with [the words adults and baptism], where would you find such a passage?

P.   I consider child baptism an old custom.

B.   That I surmise very well, dear friend; you want to violate God's and Christ's commandment in the name of custom, even though God has strictly forbidden any deviation, whether to the right or the left, from his commandments, teaching, or order. Therefore read Deut 5,[23] 17, 28; Jos. 1, 4; Kings 22; 2 Chr. 33; 2 John; Prov. 4, 14; Isa. 30. Take neither away or add to it. Read Deut. 4;[24] Prov. 14; Matt. 5; Gal. 3; 2 Cor. 2; Rev. 22.

Furthermore, you do not hold the Christian order in your congregation. You do not exercise brotherly discipline, either in terms of inclusion or exclusion [that is, neither baptism nor the ban]. You do not differentiate or separate but break the bread with everyone.

Furthermore, if someone in your congregation receives a revelation, finds a failing in you or is annoyed by your sermon and wants to bring this to public notice [the congregation] or discuss it according to the Christian order, as outlined in the first Epistle to the Corinthians chapter 14,[25] you will not tolerate it. And because you cannot contradict it or stop it with the Scriptures, you call on the temporal sword. Thus your heart and that of the likes of you is in an alliance against the souls of the lovers of truth, Ezek. 22.[26] You lack your own sword [the Word of God], Eph. 6,[27] otherwise you would not need a borrowed sword. You should gather with Christ, but instead you scatter, Jer. 23;[28] Ezek. 34; Luke 11; Matt. 12. Does the temporal authority have to judge your teaching? I thought it should be your lambs and listeners who judge, according to the word of Paul, 1 Cor. 14.[29] Oh dear lords, it is not well; you do not want to act justly and do not want us to teach openly. We do not seek nor desire any other judges except our lambs in order to remain in the teaching of the spirit of Christ, 1 Cor. 14. For those who do not remain in the teachings of Christ have no God, 2 John 1.[30] Look now, dear friend. Does it make sense that we who have come to this understanding through the grace of God could with a good conscience attend your sermons, join your congregation, praise it or call it Christian? You do not keep the Christian order but the opposite! Individual members are not permitted to exercise their gifts for the edification of the congregation; as if you alone had all the gifts. Christ wants an irreproachable congregation, a pure virgin, Eph. 5; 2 Cor. 11.[31] Yet you suffer all kinds of unclean persons in your congregation: persons who walk in the depravity of the flesh, whores, the avaricious, drunkards, greedy and foul mouthed. You should discipline or expel them, 1 Cor. 5,[32] but if they become too numerous, you should leave them with your little flock, 2 Cor. 6.[33] If you dared do that, you would (soon) discover what kind of Christians or brothers you have. They may well listen to you, but you will find only a few among them who practise; those who do practise would be revealed to us. But we cannot tell you of any Christians in your congregation and believe that you do not know of any either; nor can you call them by name as should be the case with a faithful shepherd.[34] From all that it can be surmised how matters stand.

P.   You say I have depraved people in my congregation. Friend, point them out to me so that I can discipline them, because they are hidden from me.

B.   If you can discover them only through me, then the order (*Ordnung*) and love in your congregation is poor and cold. I will not reveal the depraved to you, for of what concern are outsiders to me, 1 Cor. 5.[35] I have not seen any evidence that they have placed themselves in obedience to God and to his children. If that were the case, [if they had made a commitment to obedience], then I could well act as one should. You do not show great concern for them, otherwise you would watch over them with greater diligence and not ask me about their behaviour. You would inquire among them how things are with each one of them. You would teach and take up the [proper] order, so that at all times when a vice or depravity becomes apparent they would admonish and discipline one another in accordance with the Scriptures as is expected in love, secretly or openly, Matt. 18.[36] I thought that you would come to know members [of your congregation] at the Lord's Supper, when everyone is gathered, because no one is to break the bread of communion with open sinners, but out of love they are to remind and admonish each other of their sins and failings. 1 Thess. 5.[37] They are not to neglect caring for one another, not engage in hypocrisy with those with whom they have fellowship, lest they participate in another's sin, Lev. 19.[38] Thus, before breaking the bread they need to cleanse their innermost and outward [being]. Without such cleansing the breaking of the bread is an abomination. And such cleansing cannot properly occur without separation, for all things have their time, Eccl. 3.[39]

But, dear friend, if everyone goes to your sermon, then the door is open to everyone without qualification. It is as if one goes to a dance in an open field, an alley or at the annual fair. It is as if all kinds of cattle, horses, cows, pigs, geese, etc. come together in an open place without fences. How can you say that there are no sinners or unclean ones among them? Are we not barely a handful compared with such a crowd? Yet even though we are only twenty or thirty, we normally find one or more whom we have to discipline or exclude. How can there be none in such a big crowd? Yet you have never excluded anyone. I gladly believe you that you do not know them. How could you know them? They come to your sermon and leave again. They can easily hide their depravity from you. If you want to know them, you have to do it differently. If you had the love of God, you would exhibit a different zeal for the lambs of Christ. You would consider his commandment and the order in regard to inner and outer baptism. You would investigate and test everyone's spirit personally and not year after year talk or shout into the wind.

P.   Yes, but the authorities do not permit the baptism of adults. Therefore, we still keep child baptism as an ancient custom.

B.   Oh dear friend, how deep you are stuck in the morass of perdition. I hear well that you want to continue pleasing the world. Since friendship of the world is enmity with God, how can you be a servant of Christ, Gal. 1?[40] If you want to use worldly authority to excuse yourself, then I have already conversed enough with you. Why do you call Christ

Lord if you do not do his will, Matt. 7?[41] Yes, if you recognize that child baptism is not from God, why are you silent about it in your sermon and make yourself guilty of innocent blood? Why do you not with Peter tell the authorities that they themselves should judge whether it is right before God to obey them more than God, Acts 4, 5?[42]

Perhaps some who have remained behind would be converted to God. I fear that you are concerned with your wages, the displeasure of persons and that you are afraid of the cross of Christ which would, no doubt, follow almost immediately. Do you want to be scolded and persecuted as Beelzebub with the house father, Matt. 10; John 15?[43] Shall the servant or a bastard be above the lord, Heb. 12?[44] He who will not suffer will also not reign, Rom. 8; 2 Tim. 2.[45]

I had planned to also ask you about the inner and whether you are a Christian. But it has been revealed to me without asking that you are still far from Christian. As may be seen from Jer. 23, 14, 27, you are not sent by God but by men;[46] and as stated in Phil. 3, Mic. 3, called and ordered to preach by your belly.[47] Dear friend, accept [this criticism] for your [own] good. Take the matter to heart, I pray you, fear God and repent, change your preaching or give it up. Otherwise the authorities, shepherd and flock, blind and leaders of the blind will perish together, Jer. 14, 27; Ezek. 3, 33; Luke 6; Matt. 15.[48]

P. It was my intention to openly entice the people a little longer, a year or two, and then create a separated (congregation).

B. Yes, that is speaking according to human opinion; all you preachers say that, like Luther, as I read about five or six years ago in one of his little tracts. He also enticed openly and still has no separated congregation of God. He wrote further that if proper procedure were followed, then one should gather in a locked house and there one could proceed with baptism and other matters according to the order of Christ. And he still entices and coaxes to this day, but has brought only a few sheep into the sheep stall and forgotten the above named writing altogether, or is sorry that he wrote it. God knows of whom he is afraid. It seems to me that he now stands before the sheep stall and resists the sheep so that they do not go in, Matt. 23.[49] For that reason I am concerned that your enticing will be just like his, that you and your congregation will remain in the same chapter of John,[50] that is, always learning but never coming to the bottom of it, 2 Tim. 3.[51]

P. Dear friend, nevertheless a good improvement has come through Luther's teachings.

B. Yes, you mean rejection of external idolatry and the like. I do not call that evil as long as no other abomination is put in its place. But I speak about the improvement of hearts, a properly fenced in Christian congregation and order. Show me the same, because the soul's salvation depends on it. What [good is it] if one gets into the wool but does not get to the skin? After all, tell me, dear friend, what true love and planting has come of it up to now? Yes, this, that you want to pull us by our hair to your faith, a faith you want approved by the Emperor. Where is the love of which it is written in Matt. 7; Luke 6; Tob. 4, that that which you do not like to have done to you, you should spare others from?[52]

P. Dear friend, advise me. How should I do it, so that things are properly done in my congregation?

B. Matters are still far off. Begin with yourself becoming a Christian. Abstain from the friendship of this world, otherwise you cannot become God's friend. Completely surrender to God under his cross; look only to his will and command. Accept the suffering, persecution, and cross, inward and outward, which will result and will not fail to come to you. Such is the school of Christ into which he calls all who want to become his disciples. As one is instructed in this school and submits to God's discipline, one receives the key of David, that is, the Holy Spirit, Prov. 1.[53] Only after that may you instruct others and direct them into the school of Christ, in which up to now neither you nor your listeners have been. For this reason you are comparable to wild trees in the forest, destined for the building of a house, but you are still raw and rough, mossy, with branches, untrimmed and not yet hewn.[54] But if you do not want to go to the proper school, you will never find Christ about whom you are now divided.[55] And because you do not have him, your fishing (your attempt to win others for discipleship) will be in vain and you will forever try to climb in [into the sheep stall] somewhere else [rather than through Christ the door], John 10.[56]

P. Very well, my dear brother, I have heard your opinion.

B. Dear friend, then give me witness. Did I tell you the truth or a falsehood?

P. I can not accuse you of any falsehood.

B. Are you troubled that I called you non-Christian?

P. No, I recognize freely and in truth that I have never yet begun to become a true Christian, let alone that I should be one already.

B. Then I praise God that you have taken my opinion to heart.

P. Never before has it entered so thoroughly into my heart.

B. Well then, dear friend, consider the matter well; how it stands with you and with your listeners. Let it concern you; rest not. Consider what God will demand of you at the judgment day, Luke 12, 19; Matt. 24, 25; Ezek. 3, 33.[57] Good-bye, I am going. Farewell.

P. Farewell, dear brother. God be your companion.

B. Amen.

# Notes

[1] *The Inner Word and the Outer World. A Biography of Sebastian Franck* (New York: Peter Lang, 1994), 152-53, n.52.

[2] The Sammelband carries the signature vol. A 1208/I in the Stadtarchiv of Ulm; the tract is found on f. 690-96.

[3] *Ein new gesprech/frag und antwort zwischen ainem Predicanten und ainem Tauffer/ von wegen dess predigen/ Abendmals/ Tauffs und recht Christlicher gmain/ hübsch zulesen.*

[4] Strizell's name appears on f.697 of the Sammelband, but not in the *Ulmer Anabaptist Akten*, collected by Gustav Bossert Jr. and now in the Badisches Generalarchiv, Karlsruhe. I consulted the *Register* of the General Archiv, Abteilung S, Verein für Reformationsgeschichte (*Täuferakten*), VIII, Ulm.

[5] A fuller account of my investigation is found in my article, "An Introduction to Pilgram Marpeck's Printing Press," paper to be read at the Sixteenth Century Studies Conference, St. Louis, MO, October, 1999.

[6] "The German Mass and Order of Service" (1526) in Martin Luther, *Works* (American Edition), ed. Jaroslav Pelikan (St. Louis: Concordia Press, 1955-1989), vol. 53: 53-90, esp. 64.

[7] *Ein schöns Gesprech/ zwischen aim Edelman/ und seinem Knecht/ vom Apostolischen Tauff/ und die gehorsam der Oberkait belangend/ Und wie der Knecht sich durch den Edelman und sein Pfarherren mit hailiger Schrift weysen lasst.*

[8] Karl Schottenloher, *Philipp Ulhart. Ein Augsburger Winkeldrucker und Helfershelfer der "Schwärmer" und "Wiedertäufer" [1523-1529]* (Nieuwkoop: B. de Graaf, 1967), 86-87.

[9] *Das ander thail, wie der Pfarherr nach dem Knecht schickt, Und wie sy sich weyter mit einander ersprachen/ Von wegen des Predigampts/ Tauffs/ Abentmals/ unnd rechter Christlicher Gemain.*

[10] *Flugschriften vom Bauernkrieg zum Täuferreich (1526-1535)*, ed. Adolf Laube with assistance of Annerose Schneider and Ulman Weiss, vols. I and II (Berlin: Akademie Verlag, 1992). See especially Helmut Claus, "Druckgeschichte" in *ibid.*, II, 1012-13. Claus was unaware that Part Two existed separately as a 1532 edition.

[11] Friedwart Uhland, "Täufertum und Obrigkeit in Augsburg im 16. Jahrhundert" (unpublished Ph.D. dissertation, Eberhard-Karls University, Tübingen, 1972), 229-30.

[12] Kentner had been baptized in the spring of 1529 near Mindelheim, between Kaufbeuren and Kempten. He is, no doubt, identical with the Philipite leader Hans Gentner, who later (1537) under Peter Riedemann's influence joined the Hutterites. Cf. Werner O. Packull, *Hutterite Beginnings. Communitarian Experiments during the Reformation* (Baltimore: The Johns Hopkins University Press, 1995), 77-98.

[13] They had succeeded Hans Schneid and Hans Seifried, known to have been sympathetic to the Anabaptists. Schneid had written a letter of comfort to the Anabaptist martyr Hans Langenmantel. In August 1530 he had been arrested by the Emperor's party and dismissed from his post. Seifried had let it be known that he considered the persecution

of Anabaptists wrong. He was allegedly prepared to baptize adults should they come to him with that request. Seifried too had become a target of the Emperor's party and in 1530 he fled from Augsburg. Hans Guderian, *Die Täufer in Augsburg. Ihre Geschichte und ihr Erbe* (Pfaffenhofen: Ludwig Verlag, 1984), 72, 88. Uhland, "Täufertum und Obrigkeit," 243.

[14] In 1533-34 Wolfhart provided lodging for Schwenckfeld. Emmet McLaughlin, *Caspar Schwenckfeld, Reluctant Radical: His Life to 1540* (New Haven: Yale University Press, 1986), 166, n.25, 168-70.

[15] Riemer was subsequently active in Dinkelsbühl. Werner O. Packull, *Mysticism and the Early South German-Austrian Anabaptist Movement, 1525-1531* (Scottdale, Pa.: Herald Press, 1977), 217, n.53. On Gentner, cf. n.12.

[16] He is described as "ein Vorsinger an der Predigt." Heinold Fast, "Vom Amt des 'Lesers' zum Kompilator des sogenannten Kunstbuches. Auf dem Spuren Jörg Malers" in *Aussenseiter zwischen Mittelalter und Neuzeit. Festschrift für Hans-Jürgen Goertz zum 60. Geburtstag*, ed. Norbert Fischer and Marion Kobelt-Groch (Leiden: Brill, 1997), 191-92, ns.18, 19.

[17] Fast, "Vom Amt des 'Lesers'," 194, n.30.

[18] For a list cf. Packull, "An Introduction to Pilgram Marpeck's Printing Press."

[19] Wine from Napol di Malvasia. Cf. *Flugschriften vom Bauernkrieg* II, 1006, n. l.

[20] The reference is to Sirach 5:7: Do not delay to convert to the Lord.

[21] The reference is to Matt. 23: 25-26: Woe to you, scribes and Pharisees, hypocrites! For you clean the outside of the cup and of the plate, but inside they are full of greed and self indulgence. You blind Pharisee! First clean the inside of the cup, so that the outside also may become clean.

[22] Meant is 2 Tim. 3:9: But they will not make much progress, because . . . their folly will become plain to everyone.

[23] Deut. 5:32-33: You must . . . do as the Lord your God has commanded you; you shall not turn to the right or to the left. You must follow exactly the path that the Lord your God has commanded you . . . Deut. 17:20; 28:14; Josh. 1:7; 4:10; 1 Kings 22-19; 2 Kings 22:13; 2 Chr. 33:7-8; 2 John 1:9; Prov. 4:14, 26-27; Isa. 30:21.

[24] Deut. 4:2: You must neither add anything . . . nor take away anything . . . ; Prov. 4:27; Matt. 5:17-18; Gal. 3:10; 2 Cor. 2:12-17; Rev. 22:18-19.

[25] 1 Cor. 14: 26-32: When you come together, each one has a hymn, a lesson, a revelation, a tongue, or an interpretation. Let all things be done for building up. If anyone speaks in a tongue, let there be two or at most three, and each in turn; and let one interpret . . . Let two or three prophets speak, and let the others weigh what is said. If a revelation is made to someone else sitting nearby, let the first person be silent. For you can all prophesy one by one, so that all may learn and all be encouraged.

[26] Ezek. 22:26: Its priests have done violence to my teaching and have profaned my holy things; they have made no distinction between the holy and the common, neither have they taught the difference between the unclean and the clean . . .

[27] Eph. 6:17: . . . the sword of the Spirit, which is the word of God.

[28] Jer. 23:1-3: Woe to the shepherds who destroy and scatter the sheep of my pasture! . . . So I will attend to you for your evil doings, says the Lord. Then I myself will gather the remnant of my flock out of all the lands where I have driven them, and I will bring them back to their fold, and they shall be fruitful and multiply. Ezek. 34:2-6; Luke 11:23; Matt. 12:30.

[29] 1 Cor. 14:26, 29: When you come together, each one has a hymn, a lesson, a revelation, a tongue, or an interpretation . . . Let two or three prophets speak, and let the others weigh what is said.

[30] 2 John 1:9: Everyone who does not abide in the teaching of Christ, but goes beyond it, does not have God . . .

[31] Eph. 5:25-27: Christ loved the church and gave himself up for her, in order to make her holy . . . , without a spot or wrinkle . . . , so that she may be holy and without blemish. 2 Cor. 11:2: I feel a divine jealousy for you, for I promised you in marriage to one husband, to present you as a chaste virgin to Christ.

[32] 1 Cor. 5:4-5: When you are assembled, . . . you are to hand this man over to Satan for the destruction of the flesh, so that his spirit may be saved in the day of the Lord.

[33] 2 Cor. 6:14-18: Do not be mismatched with unbelievers. For what partnership is there between righteousness and lawlessness? Or what fellowship is there between light and darkness? What agreement does Christ have with Belial? Or what does a believer share with an unbeliever? What agreement has the temple of God with idols? For we are the temple of the living God; . . . Therefore come out from them, and be separate from them, says the Lord, and touch nothing unclean; then I will welcome you, and I will be your father, and you shall be my sons and daughters, says the Lord Almighty.

[34] John 10:2-5: He calls his own sheep by name and leads them out . . . he goes ahead of them, and the sheep follow him because they know his voice.

[35] 1 Cor. 5:12-13: For what have I to do with judging those outside? Is it not those who are inside that you are to judge? God will judge those outside.

[36] Matt. 18:15-17: If another member of the church sins against you, go and point out the fault when the two of you are alone . . . if you are not listened to, take one or two others along with you, so that every word may be confirmed by the evidence of two or three witnesses. If the member refuses to listen to them, tell it to the church; and if the offender refuses to listen even to the church, let such a one be to you as a Gentile and a tax collector.

[37] 1 Thess. 5:14: And we urge you, beloved, to admonish the idlers, encourage the faint-hearted, help the weak, be patient with all of them.

[38] Lev. 19:15: with justice you shall judge your neighbor. 1 Tim. 5:20-22: As for those who persist in sin, rebuke them in the presence of all, so that the rest also may stand in fear . . . . do not participate in the sins of others; keep yourself pure. Ezek. 3:18-22; 3:24-27; Eph. 5:1-7, 11; Rev. 18:4; 2 John 1:9-11.

[39] Eccl. 3:1: For everything there is a season, and a time for every matter under heaven.

[40] Gal. 1:10: Am I now seeking human approval, or God's approval? Or am I trying to please people? If I were still pleasing people, I would not be a servant of Christ.

[41] Matt. 7:21: Not everyone who says to me, "Lord, Lord," will enter the kingdom of heaven, but only the one who does the will of my Father in heaven.

[42] Acts 4:19; Acts 5:28-29: But Peter and the apostles answered, "We must obey God rather than any human authority."

[43] Matt. 10:25; If they have called the master of the house Beelzebub, how much more will they malign those of his household? John 15:20; Servants are not greater than their master. If they persecuted me, they will persecute you; . . . .

[44] Heb. 12:8: If you do not have that discipline in which all children share, then you are illegitimate and not his children.

[45] Rom. 8:17: and if children, then heirs, heirs of God and joint heirs with Christ – if, in fact, we suffer with him so that we may also be glorified with him. 2 Tim. 2:10-12.

[46] Jer. 23:21-22: But if they had . . . proclaimed my words to my people, . . they would have turned them from their evil way, and from the evil of their doings. Jer. 14:14: I did not send them, nor did I command them or speak to them. Jer. 27:9, 14-15.

[47] Phil. 3:19: Their end is destruction; their god is the belly; and their glory is in their shame; their minds are set on earthly things. Mic. 3:11: Its rulers give judgement for a bribe, its priests teach for a price, its prophets give oracles for money; . . . .

[48] Jer. 27:15: I have not sent them, says the Lord, but they are prophesying falsely in my name, with the result that I will drive you out and you will perish, you and the prophets who are prophesying to you. Ezek. 3:26-27; 33:12-20; Luke 6:39: Can a blind person guide a blind person? Will not both fall into a pit? Matt. 15:14.

[49] Matt. 23:13: But woe to you, scribes and Pharisees, hypocrites! For you lock people out of the kingdom of heaven. For you do not go in yourselves, and when others are going in, you stop them.

[50] The reference is to Jesus speaking of the sheep stall. John 10: 1-17.

[51] 2 Tim. 3:7 . . . who are always being instructed and can never arrive at a knowledge of the truth.

[52] Matt. 7:12: In everything do to others as you would have them do to you; for this is the law and the prophets.

[53] Prov. 1:7, 23: The fear of the Lord is the beginning of knowledge; fools despise wisdom and instruction . . . . Give heed to my reproof; I will pour out my thoughts to you; I will make my words known to you.

[54] The notion of trees suffering the artisan's work to be useful for building supplies appears in several Anabaptist writings and seems to have originated in Hans Hut's "Gospel of all creatures."

[55] The allusion is to the division between Lutherans and Zwinglians on the real presence.

[56] John 10:1: Very truly, I tell you, anyone who does not enter the sheepfold by the gate but climbs in by another way is a thief and a bandit.

[57] Luke 12:41-46: the master of that slave will come on a day when he does not expect him and at an hour that he does not know . . . . ; Matt. 24:45-51; 25:14-30; Ezek. 3; 33.

# Pilgram Marpeck's *Response* to Caspar Schwenckfeld's *Judgement*

Edited and translated
with an introduction
by
**John Rempel**

# Introduction

The *Response*, a majestic and meandering tome, is Marpeck's magnum opus. In comparison with the *Admonition* of 1542, whose substance Marpeck plagiarized from Bernard Rothmann,[1] the *Response* is an original work of sustained argument. In comparison with the *Testamenterleüterung*, an elaborate concordance on both Testaments and their relationship to each other, the *Response* is more like the first draft of a systematic theology. It is apologetic in spirit and substance, trying to answer the challenge of spiritualism with an Anabaptist understanding of the redeeming work of Christ and the nature of the church.

It was written angrily, hastily, and penetratingly in reaction to Caspar Schwenckfeld's angry, hasty, and penetrating response to Marpeck's *Admonition*. Schwenckfeld entitled his work the *Judgement*. Most scholars think that Part One of the *Response* was written between late 1542 and the end of 1544. Part Two was probably a direct continuation which was finished in 1546. The complete document is extant in three handwritten manuscripts, named after the libraries in which they were found – Zurich, Munich, and Olmuetz. There are no significant variants in the manuscripts except for marginal comments added by later hands.

Through his scholarly investigation of Anabaptism, Johann Loserth, professor of church history at Graz, became interested in Marpeck. His research led him to the discovery of one of the three manuscripts of the *Response*, and it was his great achievement to prepare a critical edition of it for publication in Vienna in 1929. That edition is the basis of the present translation.[2] Schwenckfeld's *Judgement* is also available in a critical edition, as part of the Corpus Schwenckfeldianorum, prepared by C.D. Hartranft and E.E. Schultz Johnson.[3]

## Rival Interpretations of Johannine Christianity

In order to understand Marpeck and make sense of his line of argument, we need to know his opponent and something of what he stood for. Who was Caspar Schwenckfeld, this mystical and irenic intellectual who rattled Marpeck more than any other challenger?[4] Schwenckfeld was an aristocratic reformer, initially drawn to Luther then repelled by his dogmatism and alliance with the sword. Soon he advocated a moratorium (Stillstand) on matters of church order, especially the sacraments, because they had become the focal point of hateful disputations rather than manifestations of unity.

This led to Schwenckfeld's turning from outward to inward realities as the basis for his theologizing.

He came to the conclusion that Christ's incarnation was unique in its substance and duration. In other words, Christ became human not as a member of fallen humanity but as a perfect person, with no participation in sinful reality. In his resurrection Christ, in both his natures, was transfigured; his humanity – if not entirely absorbed – was changed into the likeness of his divinity. The incarnation was not God's redemptive identification with his fallen creation, either in the person of Jesus or in a larger sense. Schwenckfeld was convinced that Christ came to rescue us from confinement to the flesh and the world of matter. Salvation and spiritual reality were henceforth given inwardly, by the unmediated activity of the Spirit. The church is that community where "heart speaketh unto heart" (Augustine) without external conventions.

Let it be said in Schwenckfeld's favour that he took this approach to the Gospel not only due to his mystical tendency but, more importantly, due to the tragic disunity of the church in the sixteenth century. He rejected all external reforming movements. As to the magisterial reformers, their fault was their rigid dogmatism and their use of coercion in matters of faith. As to the radical reformers, in particular the Anabaptists, their fault consisted in their legalism in matters of morality and church order. At least one Anabaptist leader, Hans Denck, shared this sorrowful judgement with Schwenckfeld.[5] The Lord's Supper, the meal of the church's unity, had become the weapon of its divisiveness. This state of affairs led Schwenckfeld first to propose a moratorium on baptism and communion, and later to adopt a view of the sanctified life which superseded all external forms.

Marpeck himself sought communication with the magisterial divines[6] and chastised the Swiss Brethren for their legalism.[7] His writings and conduct attest to the belief that love alone is the means as well as the end of the Christian life. In this and other convictions, he and Schwenckfeld were akin. Yet he judged his erstwhile co-worker's spiritualist conclusion to be the man's tragic flaw. Already in his Strasbourg years Marpeck had written that such inwardness doomed the very nature of the Gospel. Not only a visible church and sacraments but the Bible itself was at risk. Without a robust theology of sacred history and of the incarnation, which issued from it, what objective basis was there for revelation and the church?

## Beyond Objectivism and Subjectivism

In attempting to answer the fundamental question just noted, Marpeck found himself between the devil and the deep blue sea. On the one side lay what might be called a "lifeless objectivism," a church and sacraments whose animating principle was priestly authority. From his vantage point, it lacked both a Gospel cause – the immediate presence of the Spirit, and a Gospel condition – the existential faith of a community of believers. On the other side lay what might be called "ahistorical subjectivism," an elitist individualism of faith which despised the humanity of Christ, both in his life on earth and his prolongation in history through the church.

This is how Marpeck proceeded. He developed the same set of arguments against objectivism and subjectivism. To begin with, he outlined a theology of the church whose touchstone was believer's baptism. The church he stood for was unmistakably a divine creation rather than a human association; it was literally the extension of Christ's human nature in history. But salvation, that is, incorporation into the body of Christ, was given only to faith. It was the work of the Holy Spirit, yet humanity was not so depraved that it could not respond to grace.

Marpeck was one of the few radical reformers who had a positive understanding of ritual. In the presence of the Holy Spirit and faith – the twin conditions he always set – a sacramental action became the medium of God's activity. In that dynamic, the saving work which had begun inwardly in the believer's heart was actualized externally. Temporally they were sequential actions but part of a single essence which included the soul and the body. Thus in baptism a believer is buried with Christ and then arises to new life, as Paul writes in Rom. 6 and Col. 3. This is so because in the incarnation and the atonement Christ liberated creation, including our bodies, from the power of the devil and the fall.

Against the objectivists Marpeck leveled a "spiritualist" claim. He asserted that a sacrament did not in and of itself effect what it signified (Aquinas). There is prevenient grace, of course, but that was not the issue. A sacrament in its very nature, Marpeck contended, is the point of intersection between grace and faith. God is mysteriously at work in the world and us in innumerable ways, but he chooses to save us only with our assent. Grace is the cause of a sacrament but faith is its condition.

Against the subjectivists, Marpeck made a "sacramentalist" claim, asserting our creatureliness and God's readiness to come to "natural men as a natural man."[8] For the redeemed, he might have said with Paul, "creation is new" (2 Cor. 5:17). The subjectivists seek to live as if this world has passed away, but it is this world which God seeks to save. Thus they despise the lowliness of Christ. The promise that our bodies will rise again anchors salvation in the created order. Since we see here "through a glass darkly," we need to rely on outward evidences of God's provision for us. Jesus was that outward evidence in a primal sense; his presence remains with us through the Bible, the church, and the sacraments by the power of the Holy Spirit. For Marpeck sacraments were any and all means by which the Gospel is manifested in concrete reality, from the act of baptism to the act of loving one's neighbour.

**Spirit and Flesh**

Marpeck wrote without thinking some of his thoughts through, while contradicting other assertions. He was never quite able to achieve balance and coherence on the linchpin of his case against Schwenckfeld, the event in which sacramental reality comes into being. This is not surprising, as it involves all the fundamentals of belief: God (and his creation), Christ (and his two natures), the Spirit (as the bearer of God's immanence), redemption, and faith. The priority Marpeck places on the finished work of Christ and on its present mediation by the Spirit makes God's initiative in the life of grace unmistakable. Nor is his confidence easily shaken that God makes use of many means of grace, including bread, wine, and water. But both his fear of a lifeless sacramentalism and Schwenckfeld's probing eye for any substitutes for an inward communion between Christ and the soul place Marpeck constantly on guard.

In the recurring case study of their debate, the Lord's Supper, Marpeck carefully describes the dynamic in which Spirit, faith, love, and outward signs join in becoming a sacrament. He advances Biblical arguments for the redeemability of the created order, drawing out the consequences of the incarnation. Yet whenever Schwenckfeld thunders against the danger of seeking salvation in outward things, Marpeck accedes meekly in response that the whole power of grace lies in the believer's faith. This unbalanced reaction, which relaxes the unselfconscious unity of faith and grace in ritual found in the Bible, did not end with Marpeck. Since the sixteenth century it has been a crucial factor in the Free Churches' incapacity to develop a theology of the church and sacraments commensurate with their faith and practice.

Marpeck provides a model, perhaps even a prototype, to those in search of a dynamic unity between grace and faith, inner and outer, Spirit and matter. He presents an experiment in christological reflection, bending Chalcedon as far as he can but not breaking it.

Schwenckfeld and Marpeck both found their religious home in the fourth Gospel. John's sublime spiritual reaches drew them both into his orbit. His promise of Another Comforter was their breath and life. Only Marpeck, though not without flinching, could hold John's etherial heights together with his earthiness – with mud, flesh, blood, and footwashing. Some commentators suspect that this struggle already preoccupied the Johannine community in the first century and that only the final redactor was able to make room for that part of Jesus' teaching we now find in chapter six (and thirteen?) of the fourth Gospel. Marpeck's enduring contribution to Christian faith and practice is that he followed suit.

**The Text of the Response**

The direction each of our protagonists took diverged over time. When Marpeck re-worked the *Admonition* of 1532 ten years later, he was already sketching out the role of the Trinity in making a sacrament come to life.[9] Schwenckfeld was convinced that his friend had sold out the cause of reform. He wrote the *Judgement* as a detailed examination of and challenge to Marpeck's treatise of 1542. On the rebound, Marpeck wrote the 578-page *Response*, neatly creating 100 portions from Schwenckfeld's text and offering 100 numbered responses. Marpeck makes occasional references to these numbered responses in his text, often as a way of not having to reiterate points already made. In order to maintain a smoother flow in our text, our translation will not identify the numbered divisions, and will omit Marpeck's references to them. Marpeck worked on this book with such intensity and urgency that his style is repetitive and unfinished. One reads the *Response* for its content, not its form. Typical of their era, both writers repeated themselves extensively and used two or three nouns or verbs where one would have sufficed. In addition, Marpeck quotes the *Admonition* at length and lapses into *ad hominem* arguments against his opponent.

It is not necessary to translate the whole of the *Response* to follow its trains of thought and feel its passions. I have tried, within the limits of subjective judgement, to select a text which flows forward like a river. Where the river bed goes into endless bends, I have cut a canal through them. Where rocks have piled up – either as overbuilt foundations or as weapons thrown by our antagonists – I have cleared a channel alongside them. Marpeck's chapter headings have been removed, as have repetitions which state exactly what has gone before. I have made every effort to include enough of Schwenckfeld's argument that his voice can be heard and his intentions discerned. Direct citations from Schwenckfeld's writings will be rendered in italics in our text. My fond hope is that the reader will hear the voices of those who first spoke these thoughts, and be moved by the passion which animated them and beckoned by the truth for which they took up their cross.

This translation is based on the critical edition of the *Response* found in Johann Loserth (see below, note 2). For readers who wish to consult the original text, references to locations in Loserth will be given in square brackets as, e.g., [L. 115/*12-33*]. The page references refer to preceding text blocks. Roman numbers refer to the page location; italicized digits refer to the line numbers on the pages in question. Omissions and ellipses are noted in the conventional manner.

# Notes

[1] The critical edition of this text appears in R. Stupperich, ed., *Die Schriften Bernard Rothmanns* (Münster: Aschensdorfsche Verlagsbuchhandlung, 1970), 138-95.

[2] Johann Loserth, ed., *Pilgram Marpecks Antwort auf Kaspar Schwenkfelds Beurteilung des Buches der Bundesbezeugung von 1542*, [Quellen und Forschungen zur Geschichte der oberdeutschen Taufgesinnten im 16. Jahrhundert] (Wien: Carl Fromm, 1929).

[3] The text of Schwenckfeld's *Judicium* or *Judgement* (hereafter referred to as *Judgement*) of Marpeck is found on pages 169-214 of vol. VIII, 1927 of the *Corpus Schwenckfeldianorum*, ed., C.D. Hartranft and E.E. Schultz Johnson (Leipzig: Breitkopf and Haertel), 19 volumes, 1907-1961.

[4] The most extensive biographical record of Schwenckfeld's life and thought is that of R. E. McLaughlin, *Caspar Schwenckfeld: Reluctant Radical* (New Haven: Yale University Press, 1986). The unfortunate limitation of this volume is that McLaughlin concludes his study in 1540, before Schwenckfeld and Marpeck enter their decisive dispute with each other. Peter Erb writes a succinct introduction to Schwenckfeld and his movement, *Schwenkfeld and the Early Schwenkfelders* (Pennsburg, PA: Schwenckfelder Library, 1986).

[5] Denck was an Anabaptist to the extent that he shared that movement's critique of institutional Christianity in the sixteenth century, its emphasis on the indwelling of the Holy Spirit and on holiness of life, including nonresistance. In *Mysticism and the Early South German Austrian Anabaptist Movement, 1525-1531* (Scottdale, PA: Herald Press, 1977), Werner Packull documents the Anabaptist cast of his thought as well as his inclination to spiritualism, to the point of favouring the suspension of baptism without an explicit divine command to do so (61). He sees Marpeckian Anabaptism as an entirely separate movement from Denck's and that of the other mystics (127). English translations of Denck's writings are found in E. Furcha, trans. and ed., *Selected Writings of Hans Denck* (Pittsburgh: Pickwick Press, 1975) and C. Bauman, *The Spiritual Legacy of Hans Denck* (Leiden: Brill, 1991).

[6] The most extensive of these encounters were Marpeck's debates with Bucer in 1531. They led to his expulsion from Strasbourg. See M. Kreps and H. Rott, ed., *Quellen zur Geschichte der Täufer, vol. VII, Elsass, I. Teil, Stadt Strassburg 1522-32* (Gütersloh: Gerd Mohn, 1959), 351-61; 416-518.

[7] "Judgement and Decision," 309-361, "Another Letter to the Swiss Brethren," 362-368, "Concerning the Lowliness of Christ," 427-463, "To the Church in St. Gallen and Appenzell," 498-506 in W. Klassen and W. Klaassen, *The Writings of Pilgram Marpeck* (Scottdale, PA: Herald Press, 1978).

[8] *Ibid.*, 85.

[9] *Ibid.*, 194ff, 231ff.

# Pilgram Marpeck's *Response*
# to
# Caspar Schwenckfeld's *Judgement*

## I. Outward Baptism as a Sign of Grace

Whoever reads our testimony with an unfalse heart is sure to see what we mean and say. He will see from every passage we have written whether baptism and the Lord's Supper are a sign or not a sign and won't be able to instruct us. Therefore, let no one be led astray by the calumny and suspicion that have been cast upon us. We continue to say and testify: For the one who believes, outward baptism is not a sign of grace, for grace needs no sign; it is the essence of faith in the heart and conscience. Grace is testified to in the co-witness of the water bath with the word. Whoever wants to argue may consider it a sign. Let him show us a single letter in the Holy Scriptures of the New Testament where baptism and the Supper of Christ are called a symbol or sign.[1] Then it would have to follow that even true outward teaching is only a symbol of truth and not the truth itself.

External (*eusserlich*) teaching about faith isn't active in our heart without the Holy Spirit, who recalls to us, and leads us into all truth. It is through faith that God gives us the Spirit (Gal. 3[:3-5]). Through this outward teaching, truth is presented and offered to the heart and to the whole person. For whoever believes and is not contradicted, to him the outward teaching is a co-witness and a truth with the internal (*innerlich*) truth in the believing heart. Whoever doesn't believe the outward truth of Christ, to him it becomes a sign of contradiction leading to a fall.

And so we say that the human being Christ has been made a sign for the falling and rising of many in Israel. This is true also of baptism. For the one who believes, it is not a sign but a true co-witness to faith in the truth of the heart; outward teaching leads to baptism and faith. But if in baptism we see only water and in the Lord's Supper only wine and bread, and cannot see beyond them, then water, wine, and bread remain what they are, signs of themselves. Just so, without faith outward teaching is of no value – in fact, it is of great harm, according to our testimony. We know very well that Christ is not a sign of grace but grace itself and the resurrection of everyone who has faith. But the right and true sign of grace and love is that Christ let himself be hanged on a cross. Out of love he endured pain, martyrdom, and death. That is the sign. The One who died for us – and not his suffering and death itself – is love and grace itself.[2]

It says in our text, "As a clear sign of grace, Christ has been hanged on the cross on our behalf."[3] Please understand, the fact that he was hanged there is most certainly the greatest sign of grace. God is gracious to us; Christ is grace itself. This would be easily understood if there were no desire to argue about words. In the section of Schwenckfeld's writing which we are trying to understand, it is well to note that, as elsewhere, we mean the same thing,[4] namely, the whole work of the covenant – inward and outward – is brought together in a single covenant. In order for true baptism to happen, the one to be baptized needs first to have the new birth (in which the covenant of a good conscience consists) as the essence in the heart, in the way we have written. To be sure, we do not divide the new birth and the covenant of conscience from each other. Of course, the point of our witness, which we keep uppermost in mind, is the source of baptism – what baptism is in God's eyes, who baptizes, how baptism and regeneration started.

Just as the Holy Spirit, through faith and with faith, assures and sanctifies us, brings us to obedience, and leads us according to God's pleasure, so also our spirit (which has peace and oneness with Christ's Spirit) brings flesh and blood into obedience, with all the bodily (*leiblichen*) works of faith in Christ. They are baptism, Lord's Supper, footwashing, laying on of hands, teaching, discipline, prayer, almsgiving, and clothing ourselves in love for our neighbour. They continue through tribulation, suffering, and patience for the sanctifying and reconciling of the whole person – spirit, body, and soul – into full obedience to the God of peace (*gottes fridens*). God sanctifies us through and through and will keep us unblemished (*unstreflich*) until the coming of our Lord Jesus Christ (1 Thess. 5). In the same way, the Spirit of Christ assures our spirit that we are children of God and guides it.

Christ baptizes with the Holy Spirit and with fire; the apostles serve with teaching and water. Their service is also called baptism, but not a separate or second one or one which happens without the co-operation of the Holy Spirit in the believing heart. We say that the outward pouring doesn't depict the purity of Christ's flesh and blood in death; rather, it testifies to it – not our flesh alone but also our spirit, yes, the purity[5] of the whole person (2 Cor. 7[:1]). True baptism is to preach and believe according to the command of Christ. The office and work of the apostles is a separate matter (*unterschaiden*) but neither baptism nor the element of water should be separated from the Holy Spirit and fire. Nor should the person be divided up into flesh, soul, or spirit, for the whole, believing person is baptized for the forgiveness of sin. So we can't call water a sign, according to Holy Scripture, which simply calls it water, a mute element, to which no effectiveness may be added, according to our witness.[6] We grant those their wish who want it as a sign. Only they shouldn't make a sign out of the single and true baptism of Christ and the apostles. Nor should they make two baptisms, as they here undertake to do and to write disparagingly about them. The Holy Scriptures of the New Testament, basically and briefly, speak of only one baptism and not of any "sign baptism." We testify to one baptism for the forgiveness of sins, as there is only one forgiveness of sins (John 20). If Schwenckfeld had judged our testimony only in natural – to say nothing of Christian – love, he would easily have found our distinction between *signum* and *signatum*, outward (*auswendig*) and inward, picture and truth.

For that reason we treated the word "sacrament" as it is understood with the natural mind and distinguished it from the essence as a *signum*, a sign or a meaning.[7] And so that the poor in spirit and weak in conscience, who are troubled by false accusations and kept from the truth as Schwenckfeld slanders us, may understand more clearly, we want to reflect briefly on the places in our witness where he accuses us. [L. 112/*15*-114/ *3*] . . .

. . . Neither is it our intention to make external water by itself into something necessary for salvation. This is not to be found in our testimony. However far God's patience might reach in preserving people's bodies until they come to a knowledge of salvation, baptism as Christ commanded it and the apostles practised it is necessary. It is a bath in water through the preached word. Through such a water bath the whole person is purified through the water by faith. It is a single baptism on which salvation surely depends. See Answer 31.

Through this water bath, this single baptism, God overturns their wisdom and shows that their understanding leaks (1 Cor. 1)! Wherever they stand contrary to the truth, their thoughts are dirt and manure. Wherever they agree with the truth we shall not scold them anywhere in this book and treat them just as we do other sects. One thing is needful, says the Lord, the word of God and no other, which Christ and his apostles taught to his own. That word is contiguous with the water. When it is preached, heard, believed, and chosen you have the 'water bath in the word' which Christ commanded.[8] You can't separate one part from the other. . . . . One thing is needful: to follow the baptism commanded in Matthew 28.

> Let us pray.
> O Lord Jesus, look down and see how this generation rises up.
> They take your holy water bath, your single baptism and destroy it.
> With you and your holy commandment we shall hold the field.
> We shall triumph, gathering and sustaining your people.
> We will tell them that without the baptism, communion, and ban you have commanded, they cannot please you.
> You command baptism and do not do so in vain.
> You intend for us to hold fast to it, both for the sake of your commandment and for the purpose for which you commanded it.
> These people go against you, as if it is not necessary.
> They act in self-will, they contradict you, they scorn your majesty and your law. [L. 117/*35*-118-*26*] . . .
> . . . O Lord, if we had not understood why you commanded us to baptize as Peter, your disciple, didn't comprehend when you washed his feet[9]) – but he let you wash them, and you made him a part of you.
> This is what we need: to take things because you command them, to obey you even if it doesn't make sense, to let ourselves be guided by you, even if fools scold us and make fun of us.[10]
> How much more should we hold to your baptism, if we understand its purpose.
> Let the wise and clever go along with the world.[11]
> For the sake of your commandment and through your grace, we will play the fool.
> Let them slander, let them mock and receive their reward from you.
> Praise be to you, Lord; praise be to your commandment.[12]
> [L. 119/*5-18*] . . .

. . . The believer takes his cue from the word and commandment of Christ in all things. He is obedient in word and deed, before God and people . . .[13] Christ's baptism belongs only to believers. Philip witnesses to this in Acts 8. The eunuch desired such a baptism, that is, his faith turned to it. Philip says, "If you believe with your whole heart, you may." Thus, Schwenckfeld's comment in the margin, *that faith does not turn to external baptism and has no concern for it,* is blind and misguided. Ask him, "Where is it written that baptism has to do only with the external person?" We hold that a single baptism applies to the whole inner and outer person, spirit, soul, and body, for it is a whole and not a broken baptism. But if people could divide a person, as they divide baptism, then what Paul says in Eph. 4 would mean: Forget outward baptism. But that would be stating it falsely since there is only one baptism.

Concerning his third marginal comment, that external baptism washes away sin, that's an idolatry which Schwenckfeld invented himself. We confess a single baptism of Christ and the apostles through which (*drin*) sin is forgiven and washed away through the blood of Christ. Was it idolatry for Peter to baptize people externally with water according to the commandment of Christ and to offer forgiveness of sin in the blood of Christ (Acts 2)? He says that they should repent and let themselves be baptized in the name of Jesus Christ for the forgiveness of sins and so receive the gifts of the Holy Spirit. Peter says that; what does Schwenckfeld say? [L. 119/*33*-120/*1*] . . .

. . . Baptism is an externally offered and inwardly given truth. Before it is given, the candidate says as follows: "The Lord Jesus Christ has accomplished in me what he offered me. I attest to this gift[14] before God and those who offered it to me, as he has already attested to it in me. They ask me if I have received it and if I desire from them the witness of baptism." This kind of form is intended to make clear that the whole transaction has to do with an offer and the reception of that offer. [L. 120/24-31] . . .

. . . Hear Schwenckfeld. *"For another thing, they should explain what they mean when they write, 'The water of baptism brings no one, for whom it is only a sign, to faith and holiness.' What is it, then, and whom does it bring to faith and holiness?"*[15]

I answer: This is the exact text of our testimony. "If that is so, then let also the pouring of water or thrusting into water be a sign. We also hold that to him who considers it as such, the water brings with it no more than any external sign through which one cannot be brought to faith nor be made good. We ask you, however, what does the sign signify when the essence is not there?"[16] In response, we point to our conclusion as well as to the whole of our testimony: water without faith makes no one holy. Holiness which comes from true faith in Jesus Christ is what counts before God. (If people judged in love and were not quarrelsome, this matter wouldn't even come into question.) No natural piety counts before God unto salvation; only faith in Jesus Christ makes the heart pure and holy. With such faith baptism is no longer a sign but essence through co-witnessing, as I spelled out in the above document. Therefore, whoever takes it for a sign thereby proves . . . that the essence (which needs neither a sign nor a picture) is not yet present.

Schwenckfeld asks what is the nature of baptism. For a believer it is of the essence. As if we haven't addressed the matter, he asks who baptism brings to holiness and faith. So we will reply. To those who believe, the water bath through the word purifies. And the same faith brings holiness with it. That faith comes through the external preaching of the word; baptism belongs to this same preaching. Holiness which comes from faith calls for baptism as a witness. And by means of baptism we inquire into the holiness of a candidate's faith. If he gives a true testimony, he may be baptized. As Philip said in Acts 8 to the eunuch, "If you believe with your whole heart, let it be so." That is our explanation. [L. 120/*43*-121/*28*]

## II. The Spiritual Action of a Sacrament

Paragraph 38 of Schwenckfeld's response begins as follows: "*Let me briefly note that in the movement of grace two things, one earthly and one heavenly, come together in a believing person. Spirit and flesh are brought together in the spiritual action of a sacrament. But they are not and never will be of one essence. How can it be: one in heaven, the other on earth; one visible, the other invisible; one present to faith, the other to the senses? In the right use of sacraments, the believer raises his spirit above himself, moving from the sign to the essence, from the picture to the truth. There he remains by faith in safe haven. So it does not follow that the sign becomes one with the essence or that any object becomes one with the internal truth of the heart.* [L. 122/*24-34*] . . . *Paul writes that the internal person is renewed from day to day and grows in Christ. By contrast, the external person decays and perishes* (2 Cor. 4). *It has been said before: What these writers lack is that they don't know Christ and his new, heavenly essence well enough. Therefore, they can't distinguish the old person from the new.*"

Just as Nicodemus and the Jews (John 3:6) understood the Lord when he told them about the new birth and feeding on his flesh, so Schwenckfeld understands baptism. He insists he's not blind. Does he deliberately not want to see that we have not come to the conclusions he claims? He misconstrues us, as if we meant that by the movement of grace in a spiritual action the earthly and heavenly – on the basis of the spirit and flesh of a believing person – come together and form one essence: water and the Holy Spirit, bread and wine and the body and blood of Christ become one in the believing heart. Horrors! [L. 123/*7-21*][17] . . .

. . . The essence in the heart of believers compensates for and replaces everything which is attested by faith. It testifies to the truth that the external is together with the internal and the internal with the external. It's as if two parts of a person make up a whole person. Under the Holy Spirit, inward and outward obedience flow together. First we need a birth into purity (Matt. 23). Then the inward obedience of our spirit belongs to the Spirit of Christ, who assures our spirit (Rom. 8) that outward obedience is possible for the outward person. The appropriate body now belongs to his Spirit. Through the divine Spirit the human spirit bridles his body for servanthood and cross bearing (Rom. 6, 8, 12; 1 Cor. 9; Gal. 5; Jas. 4). The external obedience of a wholly believing person makes him – spirit, soul, and body – a partaker of the obedience of the whole body of Christ, that is, his holy congregation. He becomes a member of the body of which Christ is the head, the lord, the ruler. Each one serves the other to the betterment of the body of Christ. For in every member there are gifts of the Spirit for the common good (Rom. 12; 1 Cor. 12, 14; Eph. 4; 1 Pet. 4). What is given to the spouse (*gesponschaft*) of Christ is applied through apostles, prophets, teachers, bishops, admonishers, and the like. This is the service of the whole congregation, carried out in and through the Holy Spirit, as members grow as branches on the Vine, who gives them guidance; without him they can do nothing, externally or internally (John 15; Eph. 4; Col.2) – neither baptism, communion, laying on of hands, footwashing, brotherly love, discipline, the ban, and the like. All of these issue from one spirit to the praise of the one essence, that is, the God who is in all things, who wins us to and sustains us in eternal life unto salvation – one essence and one glory. Paul says, "We are God's helpers; you are God's garden" (1 Cor. 3[:9]). Teaching and baptism are the creaturely helps which we give to God's action. Can Schwenckfeld's sophistry claim, against Paul, that God is unable to use our help to bring us salvation? [L. 123/*26*-124/*11*] . . .[18]

. . . When our outward works come about through faith, manifestations of unfeigned love, such as gifts and help for the poor, are a union of outward and inward, so the outward carries forth what the inward begets and the inward truly betokens what the outward signifies. Or else love would be feigned; it would not be a unity – the gift and the heart which gives it would be at odds. If the heart says it has love but doesn't act that way it is false; it is a liar (1 John 4). We judge baptism and all external, spiritual actions by whether what is without serves what is within and whether the outer reveals the inner, one reality through Christ.[L. 125/*33-43*] . . .

. . . When we say, "outward person," we don't mean the outwardness of the old person but of the new one, whose inwardness and outwardness is our concern.[19] The old being has been buried with Christ, has surrendered to God in obedience, and is one being, whether its suffering and tribulation be inner or outer. Paul says, ". . . We were afflicted at every turn, fighting within and fear without. . . ." (2 Cor. 7[:5]). Concerning such outwardness and inwardness, we say what the Lord said (Matt. 23) when he contrasted it with the false outwardness and inwardness of the Pharisees. So, we speak of the true inwardness and outwardness of a believer. In that case a true external being can be well-pleasing to God – a human being whose essence includes both inward and outward, unto eternal glory in the heavens. Yet it cannot be said that there can be an outward essence without embodiment. The members of Christ's body, the people of God in essence, are bodily creatures because they have flesh and blood and limbs. Without our creatureliness we will not be saved. In our creatureliness we are saved by the grace of Jesus Christ. [L. 126/*12-30*] . . .

## III. Christology

. . . Without the revelation of the Son no creature in heaven or on earth can recognize the Father's work (Matt. 11; John 5). . . . For that reason the Son assumed human nature, to do human, bodily works – speaking words and doing deeds. Thus, physical eyes could see him, physical ears hear him, the physical body grasp and perceive him. All this the Father has placed in the Son's hands, so that the outward work of God the Son, like the inward work of the Father, is one work and essence. This is also the case with children whose birth is of God: they reveal the Father's good pleasure. . . . Let everyone judge for himself: we confess the Son of the Father as Son of God and Son of Man. The Lord calls himself a son of man. If we didn't include Christ the Eternal Word in our confession and if you could conclude that it fell into patripassianism,[20] then it would be true that we claimed to know more than we had learned from God and that we resisted a true knowledge of Christ. We have been accused of many things but when people try to prove them before God and people these things look pitiful. Christ himself is our true defender in his teaching and baptism. [L. 128/*10-30*] ...

... This is what Schwenckfeld's Paragraph 40 says. "*The fact that they do not know Christ rightly and offend his honour and office is proved by their own marginal comment, that baptism is the narrow gate to the kingdom of heaven* (Matt. 7)."[21] [L. 128/*33-36*] ... What distortion and fingerwagging he has put on paper! If you look at the whole work, you see that a single baptism is spoken of. We mention the putting off of the old sinful existence and resurrection to new life. Without doubt, the entrance to it is very narrow because we can't get through it with our old sinful life and humanity. Schwenckfeld takes the baptismal comment in the margins apart, as if we consider only outward baptism to be a narrow gate. ... Since we've been talking about a wholistic baptism all along, how can he say that it cannot be the reference in Matt. 7? The narrow gate also refers to Christ, who brings such inward things to pass. What makes the way for the flesh to enter the kingdom of God so narrow? It is through affliction that we enter baptism, through the crucifying of the old life, through the internal and external afflictions which follow from that. [L. 128/*43*-129/*9*] ... The gate of suffering is the Lord himself; though without sin, he himself went through it. It was so narrow that he comments in Luke 12, "I have come to start a fire on earth but first I need to be baptized with a baptism. How afraid I am until it is accomplished!" He offered two of the disciples baptism as a cup of suffering (Matt. 20). In sum, taking upon ourselves the cross and affliction to which Christ calls us and to follow him in it, that is the narrow gate and the small way (Matt. 7, 10, 16). The righteousness of scribes and Pharisees will not see us through this gate (Matt. 5), nor that of the rich young man (Matt. 19). Acts 14 tells us that we enter the kingdom of God through much affliction. All of this is what we entrust ourselves to in baptism into the communion of saints, as Christ's companions in affliction now and in splendour hereafter. Whoever wishes to inherit must also share in suffering (Rom. 8); whoever shares in suffering will also share in comfort (2 Cor. 1). [L. 129/*20-35*] ...

... Schwenckfeld accuses us of confused error when we conclude from this fact that the Father works inwardly through the Spirit and the Son works outwardly as a human being. Therefore, external baptism and communion in Christ are no sign but the external essence and work of the Son, to be sure, at one with the internal acting of the Father. (By "external" we mean the commandments he spoke and the actions he performed).

Ask Schwenckfeld if the Son has spoken a single word or done a single deed of what he commanded us which he did not receive as a mortal from the Father. Whatever form it took, it was also a word and deed of the Father (Deut. 18; John 5, 8, 12, 14, 17). Why does he resort to false exposition . . . ? He judges everything as it is with God the Father and before him in Christ and as it will be with all believers after the transfiguration. But we mortals live and have our being prior to the transfiguration, as did the Lord. To be sure, his knowledge is not fragmentary but ours is and remains so because we live here.[22] As long as we live in this body it's another matter, contra Schwenckfeld. St. Paul himself declares that our knowledge is made up of fragments; what we see, we see through a mirror as a dark word (1 Cor. 13). But pharisaic sophistry, carnal reason, philosophy, and clever turns of human wisdom hang before their eyes. They think they see yet are blind to the truth. Such reason must drown and sink in the meagre waters of baptism, if we are ever to be saved! [L. 133/*15-43*] . . .

. . . Schwenckfeld asks *how do you wish to prove that the Son of Man, the ruling Lord, Christ, is at work outwardly today and that he never worked inwardly either – only the Father did so.* He added "the ruling Lord" to our testimony! This is what we said: "For that which the Father does, the Son of Man does simultaneously: the Father as Spirit internally, the Son, as Man, externally."[23] That's the kind of word the Son of Man himself spoke while he still had an unglorified countenance on earth (John 5:8).[24] . . .

If Schwenckfeld recognized Christ truly, not only by his glorified, reigning countenance, but how he lived and worked on earth before his glorification and works today through his unglorified body on earth, he might understand our language better and be able to judge how we speak about Christ. Because Schwenckfeld's eye is always on the degree of transfiguration, as it is pictured above, he doesn't take seriously what the unglorified face of Christ did on earth, together with the internal working of the Father and the simultaneous co-operation of the invisible Word. Even today he works through his unglorified body (which is the church). It is the very temple of God – at work outwardly because God is at work in it inwardly.[25]

How can Schwenckfeld understand us? How can he prove that the Lord Christ is not working the same physical works now as he did then through his transfigured body? . . . His untransfigured body (understand, his church) . . . is his outward work: teaching, baptism, Lord's Supper, admonition (*ermanen*), ban, discipline, evidence of love and service for the common good, a handclasp, improving and retaining Christ's commands and teachings.[26] . . . This outward work is brought about in and through the church by the reigning, glorified Christ with his and the Father's Holy Spirit. This is openly and clearly proved in Gospel Scriptures like John 6, 14, 15, 16, 17; Acts; Rom. 15; 1 Cor. 12, 14; 2 Cor. 2, 5, 13; Gal. 2; Eph. 3, 4; Phil. 2; Col. 1, 3; Matt. 10 and more.

But because Schwenckfeld is not fond of the externals commanded by Christ or lets the wind blow them away, how could he recognize the external working and essence of Christ? It is through this working that the true members of the body or church of Christ are gathered, sustained, ruled, and recognized. The essence is the whole Christ, head and body. Let us look to our head . . . , not only in his transfigured but also in his untransfigured body, in which he was an example to us (John 13; 1 Pet. 2). The point of it was for us to recognize that we, in our untransfigured bodies (1 Cor. 6) are his members; we can follow him and be worthy of his word and calling (Matt. 10; Luke 14; 1 Pet. 2; 1 John 2). [L. 134/*30*-135/*27*] . . .

. . . Who can contradict us and say that such externality, such physically uttered truth, has not become one essence . . . through Christ with the internal truth or essence. Is Christ not still with his members on earth, present in what they confess in baptism, the Lord's Supper and other divine truth? [L. 135/*48*-136/*3*] . . .

## IV. The Sacraments

. . . Since baptism and the Supper are not signs for Christians, what else could they be but one essence with that which is inward? It is not the elements of bread and wine but the action (*werk*) in which Christ's members make use of them which is the witness and meaning of the Word of God. We don't mean water, bread, and wine, but baptism and communion.

Water, bread, and wine are not called "baptism" or "the Lord's Supper" but "water," "bread," and "wine." That is what they are. Yet if they are used according to the command of Christ, there is more to them, namely, outward words. If they are rightly used and understood, and confessed together with the pouring of water and the eating and drinking of bread and wine, then it is called Christian initiation and communion. The outward word and witness and the inwardness of faith are in concord with each other. They make a common sound . . . and a common essence. [L. 137/*14-29*] . . .

. . . Even though they are necessary, it is not the elements of bread and wine in themselves, but the action called "baptism" and "the Lord's Supper" which matters – if Christ's members are a living part of it. The significance doesn't lie in the elements; the action is of one essence with the internal. In our earlier witness we distinguished the action from the elements.[27] If that is borne in mind, there are two options. Outward initiation and communion must be either a picture or an essence – they can't be both. For the believer they are no sign or picture, as we have clearly demonstrated. The reason for calling outward actions "essences," as Eph. 4 shows, is that it speaks of a single baptism which includes internal and external, neither sundered nor split off. Christians call both together "a new essence of the Spirit" (Rom. 7), a heavenly essence (Eph. 1, 2), a rightly fashioned essence (Eph. 4; 2 Pet. 3).

What we confess with the pouring of water, also with eating and drinking, is that it is of one essence with the inwardness of the believer, and not with the mere elements of bread and wine . . . What is intended by the actions of pouring and consuming? If they are accompanied by verbal confession, thanksgiving, and proclamation . . . as they are present in the hearts of believers, expressed by them orally before the congregation, and between the minister and the baptismal candidate before and in the act of pouring concerning faith, forgiveness of sins, and the like, they are like the stories in Acts and elsewhere[28] . . . (Acts 2 between Peter and the people; Acts 8 between Philip and the eunuch; Acts 9 between Ananias and Saul). So, we don't ascribe any special holiness to the elements, but much more, to the action. It's the action, involving the heart, the soul, the understanding and to which the element is drawn which is ritualized (*gehandlet*). It is only the understanding and meaning of the action which makes a sacrament valid.[29] [L. 137/*41*-138/*24*] . . .

. . . In Christ and in his reign there are no signs, only an essence. . . . But according to Schwenckfeld's understanding, who declares himself – according to his discourse in Paragraph 45 – in favour of the annulment of outward baptism, we are blind . . . . He is undisciplined (*ungefangen*), doesn't understand us, and doesn't want to understand us. If he understood the apostolic baptism which Christ commanded and instituted in his kingdom or church and didn't repeal it; if he didn't falsely and slanderously talk as if we have already been transfigured through a bodily resurrection;[30] then he would soon see what the one, undivided baptism in Christ before God is, as we write about it and as Paul says, "One Lord, one faith, one baptism" (Eph. 4).

We know of only one baptism in the kingdom or church of Christ on earth, as we have answered herein. And even if you need water for this single baptism, we don't simply call it "water baptism" as Schwenckfeld does, for God's word and action precedes and accompanies it. For this reason, and not because of the element, it is called Christian baptism. [L. 138/*34*-139/*5]* . . .

## V. On Human Nature

. . . Schwenckfeld writes that our view of original sin is not that of the Christian church and Holy Scripture and accuses us of the Pelagian error. But he has not yet proven his accusation. We readily grant him that we do not hold to what is said to be "everyman's" understanding in the Christian church. In our judgement, Schwenckfeld and many others need to be shown that not everything the Christian church confesses is in keeping with the ancient teachers and Scripture. Among other things, there were many splits among the ancient teachers of the churches concerning this article on inherited sin.[31] Now, in our time the matter has come up again and been negotiated in various ways. Therefore, we wish to set forth these opinions and views, as we roughly recall them.

First of all, several teachers have held that the "matrimonial act of creation" (*eelich werk der schoepfung natur*) – understand, only within marriage – which happens through the conception or birth of the flesh, is supposed to be inherited sin.[32] One consequence of this view is that priests were forbidden to take women because of the matrimonial act so that they could serve the church in their office before God in purity and without sin. They were to be eunuchs for the sake of the kingdom and models for the people. Against that, Martin Luther wrote that the matrimonial act is part of the created order of nature and of God's commandment to multiply humanity and be fruitful, filling the earthly kingdom. Christ the Lord himself does not consider the attraction to marriage to be sin. For he says, "Therefore, a man will leave father and mother and will cling to his wife. The two will become one flesh. So, what God has joined, let no one separate" (Matt. 19). For God does not bring anyone together in order to sin. The matrimonial act leads to birth and not to sin. [L. 190/*26*-191/*8*] . . .

. . . Secondly, others have held flesh and blood in and of itself to be a partaker of inherited sin. In no way does this follow. Otherwise, God – far be it from him – would have created Adam in sin; indeed, he would have created sin! If that were the case, how could God fairly judge the world? How could he be called a righteous God and Judge, as Scripture attests of him (John 17; Rom. 2, 3, 8; 2 Thess. 1; 1 Tim.4; 1 Pet. 2; 1 John 1, 2, 3; Isa. 45; Jer. 11; Dan. 9; Job 34, 40). It would be blasphemy to say that God in his majesty, glory, righteousness, and irreproachableness made Adam transgress, as if God were guilty of his fall and sin. All of that is contrary to Holy Scripture: "God saw everything that he had made, and see, it was all very good" (Gen. 1).

God made nothing that was incomplete or infirm (*bresten*) (Ecclus. 24). Sin is not from God (1 John 3). Do not say that the Lord is guilty for my trespass. Do not say, he made me err. He made no one sin (Ecclus. 15). The wages of sin is death (Rom. 6). It is written, God did not make death and destruction; he has no joy when anything living perishes. He made all the peoples on the face of the earth, that it might go well with them, that they might be spared the poison of corruption (Wis. 1). And further, God created humanity imperishable and according to his image. But death enters the world through envy and the devil's grudge (Wis. 2). Concerning all this, Holy Scripture says, "I have found that God has made humanity upright"(Ecclus. 7).

Therefore, no flesh and blood is sin in and of itself; it is God's good creation. It became a dwelling place for sin through Adam's fall. Paul says he knows that nothing good dwells in his flesh (Rom. 7). It's not that flesh and blood are sin, but that sin lives in them. Through the fall of Adam and Eve the devil took root in flesh and blood through the serpent. Still today, the mind of true believers can be deranged from the simplicity of faith in Christ, just as the serpent deceived Eve with its swift cunning. She ate the forbidden fruit, Adam followed and both of them lost their created simplicity (Gen. 3; 2 Cor. 11). The wicked little seed was sowed into the human heart from the beginning (4 Esd. 4). The very form of human morals, with which we were created, was destroyed. The thoughts that came to people were in danger (4 Esd. 9) through the poison of corruption, as found above in Wis. 1. Through it sinful lusts and desires entered human flesh to its ruin and it became a dwelling place of sin. In its deranged mind human flesh fell into death and enmity with God. Henceforth, whoever lives according to the corrupted flesh must die (Rom. 8). For God looked down to earth and saw that humanity had been destroyed. This happened to all flesh on the earth (Gen. 6). We can be purified and washed clean of all corruption and sin again today through Christ and the Holy Spirit (1 Cor. 6; 2 Cor. 7).

If flesh and blood were sin in and of themselves, then the flesh and blood of the blessed virgin Mary, as the mother of the Lord Jesus – indeed, the flesh and blood of Christ himself, from the seed of David (Rom. 1) – would have to be called sinful.[33] So also the flesh of John the Baptist, the prophets, apostles, and all other saints would have to be called sin. How could they have been saved, how could a single person be saved today or eternally, if flesh and blood were sin in and of themselves? Otherwise, how could someone be set free from sins, distinguish them from the flesh itself, or purify the flesh, if it were sin itself? Is, then, flesh the wages of death and its disciple? The only alternative to this view would be the error that in the resurrection another flesh would be given to the devout than the one they bore when they lived within time. Far be it from us to believe that! This view would fortify those people who erroneously deny that Christ partook his flesh from the human generation of Mary. [L. 191/*38*-192/*51*] . . .

. . . Our witness is that for children neither inherited nor actual sin counts before God[34] because a child remains in ignorance and in created simplicity (*schoepflichen einfalt*) until it grows up into understanding (*in die vernunft*[35] *erwachst*) and the inheritance is realized in and through it. Before that, sin has no damning effect; neither inherited nor actual sin is counted against a child before God. Take note of our comment in the margins of the references given, where it says, "The origin and beginning of inherited and actual sin is in the knowledge of good and evil." When children come to a knowledge of good and evil, that is, when they reach understanding, then the inheritance which leads to damnation becomes effective in them. Then inherited sin becomes inheritable. . . . This happens to all people in their youth as soon as they reach understanding and their created simplicity dies off. Heretofore, the child is reconciled and excused for all things; hereafter, it may still hold onto the simplicity[36] of faith in which understanding is taken captive through faith in Christ. As long as this simplicity continues, no sin is counted before God until we fall again out of simplicity into understanding and sin and grow in them. [L. 193/*47*-194/*17*] . . .

. . . In Matthew 18 the Lord says, "Unless you turn around and become like children, you will not enter the kingdom of heaven." The Lord is not saying that we should in all things become like youth in its lack of understanding or its inarticulateness. We should become like children in our readiness to change direction and all those things which hinder people who have reached the age of understanding from receiving salvation. We turn away from sin through faith and Gospel teaching, by turning from what we know is malicious, proud, and in love with the world. Through true remorse and regret we disown all of it, returning, as if into forgetting and ignorance, because we surrender our understanding into captivity. We become simple, without falseness or guile, as children are. The Lord compared them with doves, saying to his disciples, "Be without falsehood; be as simple as doves" (Matt. 10). Paul agrees with that when he says, "Be innocent of evil" (Rom. 16[:19]) and again, "Be infants in evil" (1 Cor. 14[:20]). The Lord continues, "In the resurrection the devout will be like angels" (Matt. 22; Luke 20). He doesn't mean that they will be like angels in having no flesh but in the form we mentioned above, that is, children are like Adam and Eve in their created ignorance before they became presumptuous. [L. 194/*30*-195/*1*] . . .

. . . We stand firm in our confession, now as then, that sinfulness leading to condemnation follows as an inheritance only as people grow out of their created simplicity into the common, natural human knowledge of good and evil. When it extends into carnal selfish reason (*fleischlich aigen vernunft*) and the abandonment of the knowledge of good which came through the light of nature, then people stand before a judge, Jesus Christ. They do this through their fallen nature and the work of the devil. If they carry out the evil they know as heirs of Adam's fall in an understanding which is contrary to their true selves,[37] if they do not heed the fact they knowingly bear either God and goodness or evil and sin (Rom. 1) – in sum, if they acknowledge evil or sin in their conscience, that comes not out of an unfallen but a fallen nature. They have their judge, Jesus Christ (Rom. 2). God preserve us from excusing such people! We excuse young, innocent children from guilt and the remnants of their inheritance through none other than Christ. There is no more condemnation for them through Adam and Eve's fall. Nor do they have an inheritance which leads to condemnation; the wrath of God is not upon such children until they reach understanding, that is, the common knowledge of good and evil. We say, "Let the children remain in the promise of Christ until they can be instructed, until they can know and believe."[38] [L. 197/*36*-198/7] ...

... These same descendants of Adam are absolved, graced, and declared innocent before God again through the word of promise, without their own addition of faith or law. In their loins they all shared this inheritance with Adam,[39] an unwitting comfort, an heirloom, and grace: it is the future death of Christ, as the reconciler of all who need reconciliation. The children of the old age, like those of this age, have the advantage of the promise of long ago and the grace it afforded, Christ's reconciliation. [L. 204/*12-23*] ...

... As soon as the simplicity of the created order dies out in children, as soon as the simplicity of faith dies out in old people, the old Adam comes alive in their understanding and in their lust for falsehood. They become enemies of God. The serpent becomes everyone's head and the person becomes a member of the serpent's body. This serpent holds sway among the children of malice. If such a person is again to come to grace, he must die again and be buried through baptism into Christ's death, be born of water and the Spirit, and arise again with Christ through the simplicity of faith in the word. Such a one has accepted the kingdom of God like a child! As someone is born into the serpent's sway through the approach of carnal understanding, the serpent becomes his head. This happens when you come to a knowledge of good and evil and the ancient serpent establishes its rule among the children of malice, as members of its body. The evil whose source is the fallen nature makes a human being evil, carnal in understanding. Similarly, when a member of the serpent's body is torn from it through the word of grace, it comes to repentance and is taken away to be born of water and the Spirit through faith in Christ. It is baptized into one body in one Spirit. Christ is the head and ruler of his body and crushes the serpent's head through faith in him. That struggle, which is due to the enmity we mentioned, is set up between the woman and the serpent and between their offspring (Gen. 3). That, and nothing other, is what we know about inherited sin. [L. 208/*39*-209/*13*] ...

... Moses says, "Bless the children of Israel through benedictions and well wishes" (Deut. 33).[40] Deuteronomy 34 talks about the laying on of hands: "Joshua, son of Nun, was filled with a spirit of wisdom, for Moses had laid his hands on him." Numbers 37 says, "Take unto yourself Joshua, the son of Nun, on whom the Spirit rests. Lay hands on him."[41] Consider Acts 6, "They set them before the apostles and prayed and laid hands on them." [L. 212/9-15] ...

. . . We see from all this that the Lord embraced the children, laid hands on them, and spoke good things over them. He did so purely out of love for creation's innocence. Through the Word (through whom they were created) they are kept and guarded until the time of understanding. The Lord spoke in parables and figures of speech like these but they are good figures. By means of creation's innocence they attest to things supernatural and wise, namely, simplicity of faith, guilelessness, and humility. As is the case with other creatures, only pious animals, like sheep and doves, are taken as figures of faith's simplicity. [L. 212/*23-33*] . . .

. . . That is what we have to say concerning goodness in ignorant children. Schwenckfeld forgets this and labels it evil, sin, and foxiness. He slanders the divine manner, breath, and light in humanity whereby Adam was intended to govern himself and other creatures according to God's will before the fall. He could have ruled and remained holy in natural life, as he had been made. All those who were naturally holy after Adam's fall – Noah, Abraham, Isaac, Jacob, Cornelius the centurion, and others – were made that way through their immortal human spirit and the light of nature. Still today, it shines in all who admit it and creates such light or law in people in whom the fear of God dwells and leads them to natural holiness.[42] This same light shone on Adam unhindered before the fall. But after the fall, its light is obstructed by our own perverse life and will. It hinders everyone who lets it do so. In a child this light is untouched,[43] un-extinguished, un-darkened until understanding and reason appear. Then it makes its own darkness; great is that darkness (Matt. 6). The light dims or darkens through the sin and malice of the flesh. [L. 220/*14-31*] . . .

## VI. On Being a Child of God

. . . Through faith, we say with Gal. 3, we receive the promised Holy Spirit, through whom we cry, "Abba, dear Father." This same Spirit assures our spirit that we are children of God (Rom. 8; Gal. 4). [L. 281/*44*-282/*2*] . . .

. . . Further, in our testimony we say that the "mother" who brings us to birth is earthly flesh and blood. Are we in error to claim that the body or members of Christ in history have earthly flesh and blood? St. Paul speaks, "We know that the earthly frame that houses us today will be demolished. We possess a building which God has provided – a house not made with human hands, eternal and in heaven" (2 Cor 5:[1]). What house have the children of God other than their earthly body, flesh, and blood? In them they carry the spiritual treasure of being God's children throughout time as an earthly mother carries her treasure. As Paul says subsequently, we have this treasure in earthen vessels, so that the power which conquers is God's and not ours. Paul also says we are not of unclean flesh and blood (as Schwenckfeld interprets our words with his dark, even false eyes), but of purified, earthly body, flesh and blood. Through the water bath of the word, the Lord Christ purified his bodily spouse (Eph. 5).[44] [L. 282/35-283/1] . . .

. . . Again, we say in our testimony that being a child of God comes through the Spirit alone from God, but it is received by flesh and blood. Flesh and blood are born through baptism and obedience to the Spirit, rather than living by our own desires. The children of God in their human spirit, flesh, and blood remain eternally, even after the resurrection. Even as Christ was Word, Spirit, and God, he was also a human being from the seed of a woman – though without a man's seed – born of the generation of human flesh and blood. He arose according to the flesh of David's seed. Just so, we are physical and spiritual children of God and humanity; in Spirit and Word from God, in flesh and blood from human stock. [L. 283/39-49]

. . . Schwenckfeld should see to it that he doesn't make a big mistake, that is, to deny the bodiliness, that is, the flesh, blood, and limbs of the members of Christ, as if being born of God makes them disappear or no longer be real flesh but some sort of phantom. He is like other erring spirits who say, "Christ didn't receive his flesh from human generation, but as the Word became flesh on his own." The error which follows from that is to believe that his flesh was not real flesh, of human generation, and so it disappeared again. Schwenckfeld takes a position against these words, as if we were speaking of impure flesh and dead faith. This shows that he knows little and has not perceived purified flesh and blood or the effect of purifying faith through Jesus Christ. An error could easily follow from this . . . namely, that in and of themselves flesh and blood are sin. But a creation of God is good when it has been purified from sin. Therefore, you must distinguish (as Scripture itself does) between pure and impure human flesh. Schwenckfeld lacks this capacity. People like him are described in Ezek. 22: they make no distinction between what is holy and what is unholy and can't discern between what is pure and what is impure.

Concerning the discernment of the body which has been purified and sanctified, we quote from Ezek. 36, "I will sprinkle streams of pure water upon you and you will be pure. I will make you clean of all your impurities and idols." Titus 1 states that to the pure everything is pure; to the impure and unbelieving nothing is pure: both their mind and conscience is dirty. [L. 285/*21-27*] . . . Gal. 5 says that those who are in Christ have crucified the flesh with its desires and lusts. Col. 2 says, you were circumcised with a circumcision not made with human hands by putting off the sinful body of flesh. Thus, in 1 Thess. 5 Paul says that the whole person, according to spirit, soul, and body, will be preserved blameless until the coming of Christ.

On the basis of the above passages, we confess among true believers in Christ crucified bodies that are pure and holy. Thus, true believers are members of the body of Christ – flesh of his flesh and bone of his bone – the two have become one flesh (Eph. 5). Believers have not been born of blood, nor of the will of the flesh nor of a man, but of God (John 1) through the preached word of the Gospel which they believed in their heart and on which they were baptized. For the Holy Spirit (who comes through such faith, Gal. 3) gives life (John 6) and changes or renews the flesh, giving us the mind of the Spirit or of Christ (Rom. 12). Our divine birth is not of the flesh and bone of Christ in physical form,[45] as with our bodily fathers and mothers. Rather, in a spiritual manner we are of the flesh and bone of Jesus Christ. Through it we are joined to his finished work – his suffering, death, resurrection, ascension, and sending of his Holy Spirit. He has given us his flesh as a meal and his blood as a drink, that we might eat and drink eternal life from it (John 6). Through faith we partake of him, believing that his self-offering for our sin happened. Through this participation we are born of God in a spiritual manner, so that through faith and its (sic) Holy Spirit our hearts and bodies are purified and grow up into members of the pure body of Christ. [L. 286/*10-36*] . . .

. . . God prepared his Son, Jesus Christ, for us as a new and living way through the curtain, i.e., through his flesh (Heb. 10). Wherever it speaks of eating of the "flesh" of Christ, it means the same as eating of his body. In Matt. 26, Mark 14, and 1 Cor. 11 the Lord said, "Take, eat, that is my body." In John 6, it says the same concerning the eating of his flesh as he says above concerning the eating of his body. Therefore, the one statement equals the other. God prepared this body for Christ as the second Adam (Heb. 10) in order for us to be prepared from him. For God made a woman from the first, or figurative, Adam in a supernatural bodily form; thereby Eve became bone of his bone and flesh of his flesh. Even so, out of the flesh and bone of the other, the essential Adam, God made a woman, the church, Christ's bride in a supernatural form. . . . Thereby, she was made pure by his pure flesh and bone. So Christ the head and the church his bride are both one flesh (Eph. 5). For that reason, Christ loves his church as he loves his own body. Through his love for his bride, he loves himself. As it is written, he who loves his wife loves himself, for no one has ever hated his flesh but nourishes and sustains it, even as Christ sustains the church. That is the great secret of which Eph. 5 speaks. In sum, Christ the Word has become flesh of our flesh and bone of our bone, in order that our flesh might become pure from the purity of his flesh and bone.[46] [L. 286/ *47-287/19*] . . .

. . . Through his blood we are made holy and righteous (Rom. 5). Christ gave himself for us in order to sanctify our body through his holy body. He purified us through the water bath in the word (Eph. 5). We were circumcised with his circumcision, without hands, by putting aside our sinful body of flesh in which we were buried with him through baptism (Col. 2). He reconciled us with his body of flesh through death to present us holy and blameless (Col. 1). Through the righteousness of Jesus Christ, the firstborn, the justification of life (*rechtfertigung des lebens*) has come upon all humanity. Through the sin of Adam, damnation had come upon all. Just as through Adam's disobedience many became sinners, so also through the obedience of the human Christ, the firstborn, many will be made righteous (Rom. 5). He is the beginning, the firstborn from the dead, that in everything he might have pre-eminence (Col. 1; Rev. 1). He is the firstborn among many, indeed, among all his brothers, in holiness and purity. Through his body we become posthumous firstborns among his creatures. [L. 289/*3-22*] . . .

. . . Children of God are born through the word of God. There is only a single word of the Father; it comes to us from the humanized (*vermenschten*) Word, the Lord Jesus Christ. It went forth from the source, from the sun itself. Through Christ and his apostles this word came to expression through the Gospel. Even today it speaks in believers' hearts through the Holy Spirit. It is a living word, as Peter himself testifies, which was preached to you through the good news (1 Pet. 1[:25]), none other than the single word of the Father, which is God – Christ himself, according to John 1:8 and Rev. 19 . . . Therefore, Schwenckfeld falsely accuses us that we want to make two words of God. It is he who makes two words of God.

. . .

The human, bodily Jesus Christ – the Word himself, and his apostles – preached the true Gospel and word of the Father (which makes us Christian or born again) with nothing more than a human, bodily voice. They brought the good news to beings who possessed bodies. They didn't do it through angels or others from that realm (*ordnung*). Bodiliness communicates with bodiliness. For that reason, it was not an angel but the man Peter with a human voice who proclaimed the good news to Cornelius (Acts 10). It is through the humanity of Christ that the Lord exercised judgement on other human beings in their flesh, because the Son of Man came in the flesh, as is written in John 5[:20-32].

We already have partly refuted Schwenckfeld's crazy concept of "the woman's seed." He claims that lust, desire, and the affective power of the flesh were utterly removed from the pure and chaste virgin Mary and that nothing other than the word brought about her conception. Only through faith and the Holy Spirit did the word become flesh and blood, the fruit of her body. Schwenckfeld and others like him conjured up this notion. It is unworthy of a reply. [L. 298/*33*-299/*13*] . . .

### VII. On God's Rule in State and Church

Alluding to what we wrote, Schwenckfeld writes, "*It is easy to see another error of theirs concerning government creep in, namely, that a Christian cannot be a ruler or worldly regent. And again, they write that no true Christian may capture, protect, or use violence (as an earthly lord) on behalf of city, state, or people. Such things belong to earthly and temporal rulers and not to true Christians. There are other views on this matter: Holy Scripture adequately proves that a Christian can be a ruler and a ruler can be a Christian, as Peter says about Cornelius the centurion, 'Now I see in truth that God is no respecter of persons among the nations; whoever fears him and does right is acceptable to him.' I don't want to belabour the point, only to remind us of it. They err in finding fault with God's good order; that should not be.*"

The spirit who speaks here mentions respect; let's see who respects what. Concerning the notion that God is no respecter of persons, we dealt with that above . . . We did not write that no true Christian could capture state, city, or people as an earthly lord, as Schwenckfeld puts it. This is what we wrote there: "Let us see if another error concerning government has crept in, namely, that a Christian cannot be a ruler." Elsewhere, in the *Admonition*, we said: "For the kingdom of Christ is not of this world. Thus no true Christian needs to occupy or defend either city, land, or people, as earthly lords do, nor to carry on with violence, for such belongs to the earthly and temporal rulers and not at all to the true Christians, who show forth the faith in Christ. Many false people in our time have attempted, as the papists and the so-called evangelicals (as they call themselves) still try to show today, that city rulers, princes, and lords (in the appearance of defending the faith) use all earthly power. It is to be feared that they shall suffer the same fate as did those who engaged in the Peasants' War."[47] [L. 303/2-32] . . .

. . . You can see what we understand from our own words. They are quite clear . . . , namely, that no true Christian – or whatever term you choose – who lives in the light of the Gospel is compelled to use violence. Worldly authority – the sword – does, and is obligated to, use violence to rule the kingdom of this world. Therefore, Schwenckfeld does us an injustice in accusing us in our testimony of finding fault with God's good order. He will find no such word in our testimony. He should read further on in the passage we cited. The fact that God's order is misused by lords and subjects alike does not mean, as Schwenckfeld claims, that we find fault with God's order in and of itself. According to the mind of Christ, true Christians have no order or commandment in the Gospel to rule over the kingdom of this world with violence in the name or in the light of Christ. This is what worldly authority, as God has arranged it in his worldly station and kingdom, does and is ordered to do by God. We have not found fault with God's order and prescription; on the contrary, we laud and thank him for it.

To continue our commentary on Schwenckfeld's word, we say that it is hard for a Christian to be a wordly ruler. We would like to hear from Schwenckfeld what basis he finds in the Gospel Scriptures and in Christian conscience to counsel a true Christian to resign himself (*gelassen*) to carelessly take upon himself worldly authority and office. If he does rule over the things of the kingdom of this world, according to God's just and human order, how long will he remain a ruler of this world? He would have the weight of its misuses and distortions on his conscience and need to bear with them. How long would his conscience let him be a ruler? Otherwise, he would forsake his God, indeed, the Lord Jesus Christ, to say nothing of Christian patience, struggle, and knighthood. At the very least, he would escape without endangering his soul, because according to Matt. 6, no one can serve two masters – the emperor in worldly government and Christ in the spiritual and heavenly kingdom. We say that because of the limits of our understanding of earthly or worldly authority.

Now, concerning Cornelius the centurion: he held the office of centurion before the good news came to him through Christ and before he became a Christian and received the Holy Spirit. He didn't become a centurion after he became a Christian. Read Acts 10 and see that Schwenckfeld's accusation against Cornelius does not tally. And who knows how long Cornelius, who followed the Holy Spirit and his conscience after he became a Christian, remained a centurion![48]

Schwenckfeld continues: "*In the* Admonition *they write concerning the church – as it was promised to the ancients and realized in the present – that it is built upon the confession of Peter and all other believers who confess that he is the Son of God.*[49] *This is false and unjust! Christ does not build the church on Peter's, or ours, or anybody's holy confession, but on the rock which Peter and all believers confess, Christ himself. This issue arises when the Anabaptists write that the church is built on our own confession and not that of some stranger. Indeed, the church requires a personal confession of Christ from its members, but it is not built on that confession. The foundation of the church is much more glorious and constant than to be built or fortified by our confession.*" [L. 303/38-305/2]. . . .

. . . Peter's confession comes not from flesh and blood but from God's revelation: God spoke it into Peter's heart. Through God's word in his heart, Peter spoke from the heart and with the mouth. It is God who brought about this confession: it is not a human word – it was like the word God spoke through prophets and believers of old (1 Sam. 15; Isa. 38, 45, 51, 55; Jer. 1; Ezek. 2, 25). [L. 305/29-37] . . .

We know well that the rock through and on which the church is built is Christ, on the foundation laid by the apostles. But what else is such a foundation but the teaching and preaching of Christ through the apostles? They call it the word of God (Acts 15; 1 Thess. 2; 1 Pet. 1; Heb.13), which the Lord Jesus Christ himself is (John 8; Rev.19). [L. 306/24-29] . . .

How could Schwenckfeld make apostolic preaching and teaching the foundation of the church, since he more or less calls it a transient word . . . It is neither spirit nor life but merely a text, a sound, a voice. It is flesh alone, a transient creature on earth. But Paul does not call this word a creature; he clearly states that it is truly a word of God (1 Thess. 2). According to 1 Pet. 1, it is not a transient word but one which endures eternally. This is the word which has been preached to us through the

Gospel. On the word which the apostles teach and confess, on that word the church of Christ is built, on Christ himself, the foundation and fortress. [L. 306/*40-50*] . . .

## VIII. The Lord's Supper

. . . *"In brief,"* writes Schwenckfeld, *"their view is that the Lord's Supper is a bodily gathering of Christian believers assembled in love. Love, which the table guests show to one another, constitutes a true breaking of bread. You can see from this that they hold the Lord's Supper to be only a ceremony and sign of love. It is a meeting of believers to outwardly eat and drink. They neither rightly understand nor know how to discern a true Supper of the Lord in which he feeds all who have faith in him with his holy body and gives eternal life through the drinking of his precious blood. Whoever doesn't discern him aright cannot truly keep the Lord's institution. He eats and drinks unworthily of the Lord's bread and drink. Look into the* Admonition *to see what they describe as discerning the body of the Lord."*[50]

As can be understood by putting together what we have said, we question the motives that flow from the *Judgement* and the blame Schwenckfeld lays on us. Why is he writing against our witness to the Supper of the Lord? Is it, perchance, to bring simple, weak consciences into doubt and uncertainty? It's as if we don't observe communion in the right way (we get the same blame concerning baptism), [i.e.,] not according to his understanding and knowledge, and therefore not received from the Lord, but thought up by ourselves. Schwenckfeld says in Paragraphs 27, 30, and 46 that we are not empowered to observe the Lord's Supper until we should be commanded to do so in a miraculous fashion, as was the case with St. Paul. Does it follow that everything was fulfilled in Paul? That accolade is not given to any apostle. This power was not fulfilled in Paul. Through Christ and the apostles it was passed on to the believers in the form of teaching, baptism, communion, and the like. Paul boasts of the fact he received it from no human agent but from the Lord himself after his ascension (1 Cor. 11; Gal. 1). Even though the Lord did give his commandment to Paul in a miraculous manner, it doesn't follow that he uses miracles with everyone. There was none with Philip the deacon[51] when he started to preach and baptize in the Samaritan city (Acts 8). [L. 432/*17*-433/*5*] . . . In his baptismal commandment in Matt. 28, Christ gives it not only to his present disciples but to all future disciples, i.e., those who would believe in him across time until the end of the world.

[L. 433/*13-15*] . . . If no one would have been given the power to teach, baptize, or observe the Lord's Supper who hadn't, like Paul, received the commandment in a miraculous manner, it would follow that the church, along with its authority, power, and spiritual order, would have ceased. It follows that Christian faith and the working of the Holy Spirit – through whom children of God are born and the church is uplifted – would have ceased. [L. 435/*14-21*] . . .

. . . Schwenckfeld tries to accuse us on the basis of our own text that we hold communion to be only an outward thing – eating and drinking with ceremonies and signs of love. There is no way in which he can demonstrate that. Surely every godfearing reader sees that our reference is not to unbelievers but to believers in Christ. They have love in their hearts which they show and give one another. Welling up from within, it is love which compels their unity, bids them meet together in the body, and hold the Lord's communion. As we wrote,[52] no one has righteous love but Christians, because the ability to love comes from true faith . . . Unbelievers – those who lack faith and love – do not belong to the Lord's Supper. For that reason we say that it is a bodily coming together of those who believe in Christ.

If Schwenckfeld had judged on the basis of love, he would have found our testimony not only in the quoted passages but elsewhere. There he would have seen that we do not hold views of which he suspects us. We write, "More attention should be paid to how the works of baptism and communion happen and the spirit in which they are carried out than to the elements one uses." This is the clear witness of Scripture as well; it commands both – what to do and how to do it, i.e., in what spirit. Again, "Communion testifies to the revealed love of Christ, which the members of the church have for each other as they proclaim His death. And in His death, He gives us the new commandment; as a reminder of Him, we are to give ourselves for one another unto death and in His name, just as He gave His life for us out of love. Christ says that 'greater love has no one, than he give his life for his friends.' And He asks us to love one another, just as He has loved us." Yet again, "When Christians assemble, they are to be girded with love for one another, in the same way as Christ loved them. . . . The pope has in this fashion brilliantly counterfeited the model of Christ, for all that is lacking is the spirit, *love*, and truth. Therefore, even though they call it communion, it is not the communion of Jesus Christ, but rather a monkeyshine. . . . if love is missing, then Christ's example is completely counterfeited, and the communion cannot be referred to as the Supper of the Lord."⁵³ In these and many other passages of our testimony one can see clearly and abundantly whether we hold the Lord's Supper to be purely an outward matter. [L. 438/*38-439/27*] . . .

. . . In the margins Schwenckfeld quotes us, saying that Christ is quite bodily made use of (*umbgangen*) in the actions and words of the Lord's Supper, and insists that this is our communion.⁵⁴ We reply, as we have elsewhere, that this is not wrong because Christ's humanity consists only of physical speech and action. Physical reality has an effect on people because they are neither spirits nor angels. But in Christ everything partakes of Spirit and life and lasts from everlasting to everlasting. Yet Christ the human being manifests the things of Spirit and life physically – touching, speaking, and acting. [L. 440/*33-42*] . . .

. . . In Paragraph 91 above, Schwenckfeld accuses us of holding that the Lord's Supper is only a ceremony and sign of love, only an external eating and drinking without inwardness. Its inwardness consists of Christian love, which is poured into believing hearts through the Holy Spirit (Rom. 5). But in the end, he grants us that love belongs to communion – and he is pleased. You see from this that he accused us falsely of holding that the Lord's Supper is only an external thing. He writes above, there must be much more to the Lord's Supper than he has noticed until now. He has noticed love – that we believe it belongs to the Supper. So we acknowledge it, when he writes that there must be more than love to the Supper: truly knowing its host⁵⁵ and its spiritual meal and drink, feeding on it through that true faith which leads to eternal life. Further, we need to grow in new humanity through this meal and to examine ourselves to see whether or not we are worthy of the Lord's Table.

He ends up putting last things first, abusing, dishonouring, and diminishing love. Love is foremost in communion; without it there is no Lord's Supper, given what we know about love from 1 Cor. 13. Schwenckfeld mixes up and disorders the divine mystery: he places knowing the host and the spiritual meal and drink ahead of love. Knowing the host, with his kind deed, his love, his hard earned (*erlangten*) grace, and his spiritual food and drink comes first, with faith. John says, "We have known and believed the love God has for us" (1 John 4). [L. 441/*21-46*] . . .

. . . Can there be anything more in communion than love and the Holy Spirit, than God and Jesus Christ in your heart? Everyone who believes in Christ, who is born of God or love, is a child of God through the

Holy Spirit. . . . So Paul says, "Owe no one anything but love, for whoever loves another has fulfilled the law" (Rom. 13:[8]). And who could share and eat a true spiritual feast contrary to the love of Christ? Only someone who has love eats and drinks of the flesh and blood of Jesus Christ; no one else. Without such love no one can rightly offer thanksgiving.

Schwenckfeld diminishes and darkens love, saying that it is not enough for eternal life. He portrays himself as someone who can't recognize love, who hates it, flees it, and becomes its enemy. You can't find love in his false *Judgement*. So we have to prove how great and sufficient love is. [L. 443/*16-31*] . . .

. . . The Lord says, "Do this in remembrance of me" (Luke 22; 1 Cor. 11). Paul expounds this simply in 1 Cor. 11 and shows how it is to be understood. The words which follow, "For as often as you eat of this bread and drink of this drink, you proclaim the Lord's death until he comes," are to be understood as a proclamation of his kindness and of the love Christ, the host, has shown. Believers, who have been born out of this love, do likewise in the Lord's Supper. How could they then not truly know the host, him and his spiritual food and drink? How could they not know what it means to feed on him, through true faith unto eternal life? [L. 445/*40-49*] . . .

. . . A communion which is celebrated by hearts truly filled with love is the true communion of Christ. There is no other or higher basis for it in all eternity! No one can demonstrate that we were commanded to carry out a greater memorial of his love, his death, and the benefits he has shown us. These we are to proclaim and give thanks for, but also for the fact that we love one another as he has loved us. Christ himself said that the greatness of such love should be recalled: "No one has greater love than that he lay down his life for his friend" (John 15). He is our friend; he befriends all true believers in the fullness of his divine and human nature. He offered up his soul, his very life for us in death, that we might offer up our bodies in love like his as an act of true thanksgiving with everything we possess. We offer it to our Father, Creator, and God, and then to those we befriend. Not only that: we do good to our enemies, love them, and intercede for them (Matt. 5).

That is the right remembrance of the Lord Jesus Christ and the true proclamation of his death. We also give thanks for his meal, the food and drink of his flesh and blood, sacrificed for us in death. Through it we are preserved and renewed in spirit, soul, and body to everlasting life. This is the correct discernment of his body, first to hold to his very person as our head and then to differentiate his body's flesh and blood as spiritual food and drink from all other earthly food and drink. These latter feed only the body. The members of the devil can feed on that![56] We clearly distinguish the members of Christ under their head from the serpent as the head of its members. This includes the purity of the person Jesus Christ's unique body, his advent from God the Father as the Word from all eternity. He was conceived by the Holy Spirit in and out of Mary, the pure, highly favoured virgin. He took on humanity and flesh. In every way, this needs to be distinguished from all other human conceptions and births. We describe this distinction in an orderly and fundamental way in our earlier testimony as it was put in place by Christ and the apostles.[57] [L. 446/*3-36*] . . .

. . . Let the reader see and test our witness in these discourses against Schwenckfeld's accusations. He says that we *"do not consider what the memorial of Christ is, that spiritual eating needs to precede and whether, by God's grace, we have found the right practice and foundation."* The truth of this will be evident soon enough. [L. 448/*47*-449/*2*] . . .

. . . Schwenckfeld wrongly accuses us – contrary to love and truth; therefore his writing would be more accurate and true if he had written: "I wanted to find many reasons for my accusations as the basis of my *Judgement.* I found too few. But so that everyone may see that I am no baptism brother, and because they assert the truth over against my notions, I had to write the *Judgement.*" If he had done such a thing, Schwenckfeld would have written and spoken the truth and judged himself justly and well.

Schwenckfeld tries to deduce a peculiar wisdom from Saint Paul, as if no true believer who glories in his faith (by grace we do not deny that we have such faith) has the wisdom and understanding of the Holy Spirit in communion. All of us who believe in the truth have this wisdom and understanding through the Holy Spirit, whom we have received through faith (Gal. 3). I wonder if Schwenckfeld himself understands the words referred to in Paul [1 Cor. 10] and has taken them to heart (to the wise I say, mark my words). We leave judgement to those who are wise in the Spirit.

Paul's words take note of the mixture of believers with unbelieving Gentiles. He wants to distinguish their communion (*gemainschaft*) from that of the Gentiles. Believers should be shrewd and know that they can have nothing in common and have no communion with sacrifices to idols. In his speech to the believers he commands them to judge whether what he is saying is possible or not. And so he says, "Therefore, my beloved, flee idol worship. I'm speaking to the prudent: judge what I say. The cup of thanksgiving, with which we give thanks, is it not the communion of the blood of Christ? The bread which we break, is it not the communion of the body of Christ? For we, who are many, are one bread and one body, since we are all participants in one bread." He continues on the same theme. That is also our understanding, which we hold and discern in the same way: you cannot have a communion of idol worshipers together with a communion of the body and blood of Christ. [L. 449/*16-48*] . . .

. . . Our baptism and Supper are based on the above-mentioned action and effect of God, Christ, and the Holy Spirit (whether inward or outward effect). They come from faith as God's just work. Inwardly, Christians are made holy and moved by the Holy Spirit; their life is hidden with Christ in God (Col. 3). No creature in heaven or on earth may judge that life. Through the Holy Spirit that life comes to outward expression, revealed in the flesh and through the body for obedience to the word, to which we testify before the world. . . . Through faith in Jesus Christ we become holy in heart and spirit; in the flesh – with our mouth – we make confession and are saved (Rom. 10). This happens externally, in the flesh as the external word of teaching or preaching, as well as baptism, the Lord's Supper, admonition, discipline, punishment, the ban, and more. It brings about the salvation of the confessor and others, just as Jesus and the apostles first brought salvation to humanity.

Further, our understanding of "the word of the Lord" is that everything depends on the Holy Spirit who makes us alive and holy (only the Spirit can do this). What holy people do in faith is God's work.[58] Among the outward works believers do is make use of bread and wine; they eat and drink for the remembrance of Christ. Our communion takes form in bread and wine just as our baptism does in water. Because of that, we say simply that we are commanded to eat bread and drink wine. [L. 452/*41-453/20*] . . .

. . . We use bread, wine, and water for the Lord's Supper and baptism, but bread, wine, and water are and remain elements; they are creatures, and do not become the essence itself. . . The point is that Christ commands us to make use of them in communion and initiation. Such elements and creatures are not in and of themselves, nor in their use, the Supper and baptism themselves, even as you can't call "food" itself a "banquet." It is not a meal without the guests; the guests make the meal and use food to bring pleasure. No meal without the guests; no guests without the meal.

Just so, the water is not the bath, but you need it in order to bathe. So you can't bathe or wash without water. Even as these things have a use in nature, so believers use them naturally (because they still live in the natural state), but bound . . . to the supernatural eternal essence and spiritual working of God in the whole person, inward and outward. Otherwise the undivided person – inner and outer – could not be saved through Christ as spirit, body, and soul. You can't prove from this that we're making a creature into God and God into a creature, as Schwenckfeld has accused us. We have already answered his 50th and 51st statements.[59] [*L. 454/3-24*] . . .

. . . In the *Admonition* we wrote, "Alas, for a long time a contradiction has prevailed: many have wracked their brains and presumed, with great quarreling, to prove what the bread and wine, the communion is. One of them makes a certain claim; the next one makes another." In the *Admonition* we wrote against the understanding the Thomists, Papists, and Lutherans have of the words "this is my body; this is my blood."[60] We wrote against their writings in which they hold that after the speaking of the quoted words the bread and wine are the body and blood of Christ or something like it. In the *Admonition* we say, "Paul and the other apostles do not place a high value on the elements and, indeed, attribute no special holiness to them, but much more the action and usage."[61] We continue to say this now. So you see that both of them, baptism and the Lord's Supper, are called sacraments.

You can read further in our testimony that we do not destroy the words of Christ, "this is my body; this is my blood," nor make out of bread and the body of Christ a single essence or make a creature into God.[62] We clearly lay out our sense and understanding of these same words without fogginess or misuse. In the *Admonition* we say of the bread and wine that it is no more than an external watchword.[63] The power and potency that prove effectual lie only in the heart of each person. Based on our earlier witness, as Schwenckfeld himself attests, the breaking of the bread and the drinking of the cup by believers is a true communion of the body and blood of Christ according to the Lord's understanding and to a supernatural, spiritual perception. This may be found in a section which Schwenckfeld left out. "If you, with all your heart, are infused with love of Christ and your neighbour, if you are inclined with all your heart to demonstrate the example of Christ to your brothers – and not only your brothers but also strangers and enemies according to the words of the Lord Jesus – then the breaking of the bread and the drinking of the cup is a true communion of the body and blood of Christ.[64] But if your heart is full of guile, envious, unkind, or embittered toward your neighbour and you do not repent with true remorse, then you eat and drink the bread and wine to your own judgement. Therefore, the whole potency lies in the human heart[65] and not in externals like bread and wine." We've said this already in Answer 52 above. There and elsewhere you can clearly see that we judge the breaking of bread which Christ commanded according to the true understanding, that is, spiritually, according to the content of faith and spiritual perception – in a supernatural, spiritual manner and form. [L. 454/*33*-455/*25*] . . .

. . . Even so, in the breaking of bread – which is commanded – we look only to that which is witnessed to through natural elements like bread and wine; the teaching and preaching of the word attests to the fact that just as natural bread and wine give the body of the believer food and drink for this mortal life, so also, he is fed in his soul or through faith to eternal life with the flesh, body, and blood of Jesus Christ, believing that such a body of Christ's flesh and blood was given over to death and shed for his sins.

In these and other forms the creatures that Christ mandates (though in themselves they are and remain creatures) succeed, through the spiritual use made of them and through the understanding of faith, in making the breaking of bread and the drinking of the cup into a true communion or participation in the body and blood of Christ. He brings it about in truth (*warhaftig dran hat*) and it is an outer and inner, a single communion (just as we said of baptism). Yet bread and wine remain what they are, namely, mere creatures; by themselves they are not the Lord's Supper.

Although Schwenckfeld doesn't point to chapter and verse, "the external eating is a true internal communion of the body and blood of Christ," we stand by the claim (bearing in mind our circumstances) that the external eating of the above mentioned forms (*gestalt*) is a true, inward communion of the body and blood of Christ – a true communion of believers to eternal life, including their whole humanity, spirit, soul, and body. This, and nothing else, is what Paul means in 1 Cor. 10 and what is attested to in other places of the holy, evangelical, apostolic Scriptures.

Because of that we have already quoted Sebastian Franck's reasonable understanding in his *Chronicle*, "Paul called the bread a participation in Christ's body, and the cup a participation in Christ's blood. The bread and wine are not the essential part. Rather, those who eat of it testify thereby that they believe they are also having communion with

Christ in the way mentioned above."⁶⁶ Our own writing in this vein is a refinement of the above and nothing else.⁶⁷ . . . And we have not forgotten how Schwenckfeld earlier accused us falsely, out of an envious heart. That is not contrary to our earlier meaning but in accord with it. We wrote, "But the symbols or tokens of remembrance dare not be the same as that which they represent, or that which one memorializes with them."⁶⁸ [L. 457/7-47]
. . .

. . . Outward baptism and communion have been referred to in this book as "signs" and "symbols" or "figures" in form and mass, as we conceived of it. We repeat, where the truth is in the heart as the essence (that is the significant thing), there the signs and figures as elements and creatures are no longer mere signifiers. They are no longer signs and figures of this faith in Christ but co-witnesses and essence with the inner essence of the above forms. Understand, they are not one with the essence according to their creatureliness – they don't become the essence but remain what they are, namely, water, bread, and wine – but according . . . to their meaning, sense, and understanding, as said above.⁶⁹ In Christ there is only essence and truth, not sign or figure, as we have often said. Similarly, the inner and outer Word of God . . . is only a single essence to the true believer in sense, understanding, and meaning. The same is true for the outer and inner baptism and Lord's Supper.

There is one difference between outer baptism and Lord's Supper as they were instituted by Christ. The believer needs outer baptism only once, namely, his entry into Christendom or into becoming a Christian. But communion should be used or held often – not as a sign or figure but as a co-witness and essence with the inner essence of the heart. If a believer becomes careless and forgetful of the inner essence and memorial of Christ – his death and benefits; if he no longer knows how his heart should be disposed, for him it is mere bread and wine. In the Lord's Supper we use a figure and token of memory to recollect, challenge, amend, revivify, and edify our hearts. Where we don't make amends, we participate in the action of the bread and wine of the Supper to our own judgement, according to the words of Paul in 1 Cor. 11.

To summarize, to the extent that a Christian lacks the inner essence, to that extent the bread and wine of the Supper are only a figure or sign. But with such form and discrimination communion is both: an essence and a figure and sign. When Christ observed the Supper with his disciples, it was only a figure and sign and not the essence. It couldn't be because that which it symbolized – the self-offering of Christ's body and blood in death – had not yet been accomplished. That is, they couldn't yet eat and drink his body and blood. The meal had not yet been cooked; the blood had not yet flowed forth until the Lord hung on the cross, died, arose, ascended to heaven. He had not yet sent the longed-for Holy Spirit to recall to us participation in such food and drink through the apostolic preaching.[70] He said, "Eat, this is my body, which will be broken for you" (1 Cor. 11).[71] Understand his words; he says "which will be broken" and not "which is broken," because he was not yet broken. When he would be broken, they should eat of it. Therefore, Christ gave them bread and wine only as a figure, or, body and blood under the name (*titel*) of bread with hidden, figurative speech or parabolic words. But it didn't happen essentially in the heart until after his ascension.[72] Thereafter, he spoke no longer to the true believers through figures of speech or parabolic words but through the Holy Spirit, who freely recalls what is essential, in the hearts of believers (Matt. 13; John 16). ... He also said in John 14, that the Holy Spirit, whom his Father would send, would teach them all things and recall to them everything he had said to them. In addition, there is John 16:[13-15], "When the Spirit of truth comes, he will lead you into all truth; he will not speak about himself, but what he hears, that he will speak. He will proclaim to you that which is yet to come; he will take it from me and proclaim it to you."

Today, after his ascension, the Lord speaks freely through the Holy Spirit, the Spirit of truth, in our hearts, recalling and teaching, so that we can recognize, know, and understand the sense of his words on communion and other matters. John says, "You have the anointing of the Holy One and know all things." You do not need to be taught, but whatever the anointing teaches you, that is true (1 John 2[:20]). [L. 458/*22*-459/*33*] ...

The words of Christ are all truth, spirit, and life, the right way and guide to salvation. Only the unbelievers, the unrepentant, the insecure, the comfortless and loveless – those who have not yet been freed, who do not have the Holy Spirit's witness in their consciences and hearts[73] – do not need to obey the words and commandment of Christ. ... When true believers make use of outer things but do so with an insecure conscience, their own insecure conscience condemns them. But for true believers the use of outer things is joy, peace, and comfort – their delight in sorrow, suffering, and remorse for sin. They receive forgiveness unto salvation and assurance through the Holy Spirit, the sure pledge of their heart. ... They rejoice in the presence of all creatures and witness to the teaching of their

Lord. . . . They call out to him, to the physician of their soul and conscience, that he might become known before all people unto their salvation and the praise of their physician and Lord. How can an invalid, with an uncertain conscience and fear of his medicine, praise the physician or his skill? Such a one frightens others (who have sickened and died through their sin) and does not sing the praises of the physician's skill and medicine. Take the man born blind in John 9, badly born according to carnal reason. He did not scorn Christ's command to take the mud mixed with spittle and wash himself in the lake of Siloam. He did what the Lord asked. [L. 461/*15-37*] . . .

. . . By God's grace we know about the spiritual food in the Lord's Supper, which Schwenckfeld mentions above. We do not doubt that we do not (sic) believe rightly concerning it.[74] From our earlier testimony . . . it is clear how we understand the body, flesh, and blood of the Lord Jesus Christ as offered up and shed for our sins. The Lord Jesus Christ spoke to the Jews concerning the kind of food he gives us. "Do not labour for the food which perishes, but for the food which endures to eternal life, which the Son of Man will give you." And again, "The bread which I will give is my flesh, which I shall give for the life of the world" (John 6[:27,51]).

We know the bread well, which God the Father gives from heaven, as the Lord said, "My Father gives you the true bread from heaven. For this bread is the bread of God which comes from heaven and gives life to the world." The bread of heaven is the Lord himself, according to the Spirit and the Word, as he himself says, "I am the bread of life. I am the living bread, come down from heaven. Whoever eats of this bread will live in eternity" (John 6). Such bread has given us and all true believers life; it continues to do so, as we wrote. The Lord's flesh is the true food and his blood the true drink, which he, the Son of Man, gave for our life. Through faith he preserves the Spirit and the Word he has given. It is this meal which will make possible the resurrection of the body through Christ on the last day (John 6). We confess that in like manner the Lord will give food and drink to the soul, to the inward person, with his holy flesh and blood. The food and drink for spirit and soul must be spiritual; natural bread and wine do not nourish the soul. But they are used as a remembrance and proclamation of Jesus Christ's death and as thanks for it in a spiritual manner. They sustain the inner person, soul and spirit. Through them our body has hope, coming from within, expressing itself without, in the resurrection of the body to eternal life and in thanksgiving to God.

Therefore, the whole, undivided person – spirit, soul, and body – is fed and preserved until the resurrection of the body to eternal blessedness. The Word and the Spirit accomplish this through faith and baptism.[75] [*L. 467/ 10-46*] . . .

## IX. Christology: the Humanity and Divinity of Christ

For the love of Christ we want to hold fast to grace. We know love because we have tasted the friendliness of God and Christ and know that it is good. In love God forgave our sins for the sake of Christ. We know that God will never count them against us because Christ gave up his life for us (1 John 3). We develop a taste for his love – that's why his Supper tastes so good! For this reason, as we say in our testimony, it becomes a loving Christian meal, whose watchword is the unfeigned love of believers, which we have for Christ's sake. Thus, we do properly recognize Christ in his glory and honour. Listen to our witness. "He is a true, natural human being of the lineage and seed of David and offered up his natural life and body for us in death."[76] Paul and Scripture say the same thing. Schwenckfeld thinks he can show us how to speak of such matters. . . . He should diligently take his own opinion to heart. He intends to show honour to Christ; he, in deep humility, does not want to rob Christ of his honour. But the outcome is . . . that neither he nor his compatriots can rightly judge the meal and Supper of Christ. They do not know where to find the food; they haven't tasted or touched it. . . . In sum, we notice and sense why Schwenckfeld always accuses us that we have neither knowledge, nor understanding, nor recognition of the meal in the Lord's Holy Supper. His words about Christ in his glory bear witness that he looks upon spiritual food differently than we do. He says we cannot know it unless we rightly recognize Christ in his glory. It is worth noticing that he means the transfigured body, as it is after the ascension, sitting at the right hand of the Father. This transfigured body, flesh, and blood is the food of communion. [*L. 470/47-471/29*] . . .

. . . In Schwenckfeld's "On Knowing Christ" it says, "*Some would say Christ is with us only according to one nature and through his Spirit. His body is not true food nor his blood true drink, unless we believe that his body was given up for us into death and his blood was shed on the cross for us. They should be faithfully exhorted to further examine this secret, that they take care not to tear apart the single, unitary Christ. They tear Christ apart, they have half a Christ in their heart, or worse, take their own thoughts about Christ to be him. They confine his human nature to a* *physical location; they want only the one nature of Christ. They should ponder their views concerning the reign of the human being, Jesus Christ. What do they make of it? Can the Spirit of Christ, without the presence of the whole Christ, be with us? Should he be separated and divided, so that a physical medium (in which the person Jesus remains, circumscribed by the physical dimension) comes in between? That means he is given a carnal (*fleischlische*) form. Think about it!*"[77] [L. 471/34-472/12] ...

The writings set out above were taken from the aforementioned booklet of Schwenckfeld. Later on I will include pieces from this and other booklets, such as "Vom Worte Gottes" (Concerning the Word of God) and "Creaturlicheit an Jesu Christo" (The Creatureliness of Jesus Christ). We do this in order to understand what and how he writes, and for what reason he claims the transfigured body, flesh, and blood of Jesus Christ as the soul's spiritual food and drink in the Lord's Supper. He takes the food and drink to which we have witnessed above, and ignorantly and imprudently accuses us. We consider this plea and accusation to be an error, indeed, a gruesome defection from the truth, a remarkable robbery of the true food and drink of communion. It weakens receptive hearts which are pregnant with faith in Christ. It darkens the right faith that belongs to baptism and the Lord's Supper – that faith which fits with apostolic practice. Through it we are reconciled to God, receive the gifts of the Holy Spirit as comforter, and enter into the communion of saints or church of Christ.

For whoever would enter the church of Christ must be driven by spiritual hunger and thirst, namely, a hunger and thirst for God's grace and comfort, for mercy unto the forgivenness of sins and the laying aside of God's wrath, after being made devout and righteous before God. Matt. 5, Luke 1, John 7, and Isa. 55 talk about this hunger and thirst. It comes when we recognize our sins and their wages: eternal death, in which people get stuck. People need to recognize their sins and eternal death and know the burden which comes with this recognition (Matt. 11, 9; Luke 5; ). ... They need to have a broken and crushed heart (Isa. 57, 66; Luke 4) and perceive within them the fact that sin will bring eternal death and lostness (Rom. 7; Matt. 10, 18; Luke 15, 19). And they must have such a hunger and thirst that they will make use of the baptism which Christ instituted and commanded. Anything else is of no avail. Only the sick and the dead, only the hungry and thirsty of soul, take the soul's medicine. [L. 481/*11-40*] ...

... When they hear of this medicine – the fact that the Lord Jesus Christ gave his body, flesh, and blood for their sins – they believe it.

Through it their hunger and thirst are stilled and they are restored from sickness and death. . . . Through faith they receive the promised Holy Spirit (Gal. 3; John 7), who comforts, reminds, and guides them into all truth, as in John 14, 15, 16, 17. The Spirit brings them to life from eternal death (John 6; Rom. 8). The words of Christ, which describe how, by faith, we enjoy the flesh and blood he offered up, are Spirit and life in the believing heart. We live by it, as we do by every Word of God (Matt. 4; Luke 4).

For such a believer, apostolic baptism pertains to the washing away and forgiving of sins through the shed blood of Jesus Christ. Such believers make the right use of the baptism and communion which Christ instituted and give thanks for food and drink of the soul. The flesh and blood of Jesus Christ is not transfigured and immortal but mortal and untransfigured, as he offered himself up and poured himself out to reconcile our sins before his resurrection and transfiguration. Right after his resurrection he was transfigured and glorified but he didn't submit to death on our behalf in a transfigured state.[78]

Apostolic baptism is for the forgiveness and cleansing of sins, for making us righteous and devout through the shed blood of Christ. So also is the faith of the baptismal candidate (as an entry to the whole Christian faith) a faith unto forgiveness and righteousness (*gerechtmachung*) through the death of Jesus in his humanity before his resurrection and glorification. . . .

This is true also of the Lord's Supper. We are strengthened and refreshed through the faith which we received before baptism through Christ's death for humanity's sin. . . . The command of Jesus Christ attests to this: that we should remember the benefit of his death and proclaim it with bread and wine until he comes. He did not say the presence of his transfigured and immortal flesh, but his death. We are to understand "until he comes" as his bodily coming, because through the Holy Spirit – or his divine nature[79] – he is already present to faith (Gal. 3; John 7) with and in the believers in the Holy Supper, and at all times. For that reason the little words "till he comes" and others like them attest to the fact that he is not yet bodily present in his transfigured body, flesh and blood.[80] And if those little words, "till he comes," overpower Schwenckfeld and wrestle him to the ground, may he grasp how his booklet has gone wrong in claiming that the transfigured body, blood, and flesh are present in communion and are eaten and drunk as the right food and drink. That simply can't be found in those little words. The sick, hungry, and thirsty soul finds food and drink in the Lord's Supper, as it has already found life and righteousness, refreshment and sustenance, in baptism. This it finds by faith in the words and proclamation of Christ's death, that he offered up his flesh and poured out his blood for it. This food and drink alone is what the soul tastes in its hunger and thirst. Therefore, the words which describe our enjoyment of Christ's offering for our sin are spirit and life, in and through faith (John 6). Then we are exempt from eternal death. We are alive and receive the holy, lifegiving Spirit . . . (Rom. 8; John 6).

As we have said, life-giving and sin-forgiving faith focuses on the time and history of Christ's death for the forgiveness of sins and the offering up of his untransfigured body, flesh, and blood. Only this death . . . feeds, strengthens, and consoles the mourning soul and conscience through faith. The flesh and blood of Christ, which was offered up in death, is the right food in the Lord's Supper. According to the Lord's words, "The bread which I shall give is my flesh, which I shall give for the life of the world" [John 6:51].[81] It's clear that the flesh and blood which the Lord Jesus Christ bade us eat and drink was his untransfigured mortal body and blood unto reconciliation and favour with God . . . . It is not the transfigured, spiritual, exalted, flesh and blood! According to Eph. 4 and John 16, Christ ascended and went to the Father to reach for the gifts and graces he had attained.[82]

We are reconciled through the death of the untransfigured body, flesh, and blood of Christ and not the life of the transfigured Christ (Rom. 5; Col. 1). The Lord said it is the Spirit who gives life; the flesh is of no avail (John 6). There he says – as the Jews and disciples both tried to do – that physically eating his flesh is of no use in gaining eternal life. The Lord makes no distinction between his untransfigured and transfigured flesh, but speaks without distinction of his "flesh." It is not a matter of physical eating, as his disciples and audience understood in his discourse on eating his flesh. They thought he meant they should eat it physically. Therefore, people made reference to his transfigured body, since physical eating is of no avail. For that reason he didn't give it to be eaten physically. . . . What matters is that he is our high priest and mediator. . . . He is our throne of grace, our representative, and sender of the Holy Spirit. When he says that it is the right food, he means it spiritually, to be eaten in faith, as we have testified above. If Schwenckfeld's opinion were true, the Lord must have made a distinction, saying, "my untransfigured flesh is of no avail."

According to Christ's words it follows that eating his flesh physically, even in its transfiguration, is of no use.[83] . . .

The Lord said in John 6 that the Holy Spirit whom he would send, would bring life through calling to mind and distributing the possessions and gifts we have gained through the death and flesh of Christ. There is nothing life-giving in eating his flesh physically. Spiritual eating feeds and comforts sorrowful and hungry souls who believe that to ransom life he gave himself and now sits at the right hand of God as our mediator, advocate, and high priest. Through that kind of eating comes life and redemption from death. Our salvation came about through Christ's untransfigured body, flesh, and blood, that is, through his accepting death on our behalf. We feed on him unto our reconciliation from sin and the wrath of God. His transfigured body couldn't have helped us. Everything would have been in vain as regards salvation: he would have gone to the Father without bearing fruit, and the grain of wheat would have remained alone (John 12). Even today, when someone claims that Christ's transfigured flesh and blood is with and in us, that it is the food and drink of the soul in communion, it is of no help. All that matters is to believe that Christ's untransfigured flesh and blood was offered up for our sin. Without that faith, grace cannot reach down to people and grant them eternal life. Without it we would not be reconciled; we would have neither a half nor a whole Christ![84] [L. 481/*45*-484/*5*] . . .

. . . The true bread, which Christ gave us and bade us eat, did not come from heaven but from the Virgin Mary, in untransfigured and mortal form.[85] His transfigured form will come on the day of judgement, according to Scripture. But the bread which comes from heaven in the meanwhile, until the future Lord's body descends, is the bread which God the Father sent down and still gives. The Lord himself said, "My Father gives you the true bread from heaven, for this bread is God's bread, which comes from heaven and gives life to the world." It was bread from heaven for the Lord Christ was from eternity, as Spirit, Word, and in his divine nature. Hear him, "I am the bread which comes down from heaven," and again, "I am the living Word, come from heaven. Whoever eats of this bread will live forever" (John 6).[86]

Even now Christ is here according to the flesh and according to human nature; they have been taken up into God of very God, who is Spirit (*in Gott einkommen und Gott in Gott ist*). Therefore, Christ's flesh is also God, as it is also the Holy Spirit, in the oneness of the Trinity, a lifegiving power yet without annulling his true humanity and flesh. His two natures, forms, and characteristics are united in one. This is how we may understand Paul's verse, which pleases all true believers, "the Lord is Spirit" (2 Cor. 3). If believers in Christ who abide in God, who himself is Spirit, are called "spirits" (1 Cor. 6; Heb. 12), how much more the transfigured, divinized, spiritualized human being Jesus Christ?

In his booklet, "Concerning the Knowledge of Christ," Schwenckfeld takes the verse, "the Lord is Spirit," and rightly applies it to the transfigured flesh and human nature of Christ, but not according to our meaning. ... He wants Christ, in his divine nature, to be everywhere, and also to be everywhere in his human nature, namely as spiritual food in the Lord's Supper.[87] In our various writings we have not been able to find that Christ, according to his human nature, body or flesh, is what he is according to his divine nature. If this were the case, his human nature – his very flesh and blood – would be lost. [L. 484/*47*-485/*29*] ...

... As is the hunger and thirst, so also the food and drink, fashioned to slake our hunger and thirst. It is the sweetest and most savoury fare. ... To eat it in any other way than we have described above is in vain. We partake of the whole Christ and not half a one, as Schwenckfeld thinks. He accuses us of an unjustified differentiation of the body of Christ in his ninety-first discourse. But ours is the correct distinction. All who believe that Christ became flesh and blood, that he offered himself up to reconcile our sins, are the body and members of Christ. Subsequently, at the last day, the transfiguration of his body through the resurrection will become part of our body, even as has been shared with us in this age of grace, because through faith, we are the body of Christ now. Subsequently, the transfiguration of his body through his resurrection from the dead will become part of our bodies on the last day, even as in this age grace has become part of us. Through faith we are now the body of Christ. That is where the right distinction lies between the body of Christ and the body of the devil and this world.[88] [L. 487/*9-25*] ...

... The Lord, the human being Jesus, is God himself, according to his Spirit or inner person. He inbreathed Adam so Adam became himself (*einblaser des Adams in Adam*). So, it follows that even in the human bodiliness of Jesus Christ, whom we described as the body of God, he has all the divine, if now invisible, features: eyes, ears, hands, arms, fingers, virtues, understanding, and wisdom which God the Father has possessed in eternity! Through the Word fully made flesh and through the transfiguring of the flesh of Christ all his members are fully alive in his humanity. [L. 496/*20-28*] . . .

. . . The eyes and face of Christ's transfigured humanity are described in Revelation. . . . In the middle of the elders stood a Lamb, as if it had been slain. It had seven horns and seven eyes, which are the spirits of God sent into all lands. Like it is the transfiguration of Christ, in which the Word as Godhead permeated his mortal humanity with divine brilliance. His face shone like the sun and his clothes were as white as snow (Matt. 17; Mark 9; Luke 9). Peter describes the transfiguration in retrospect, "We have seen him in his majesty, we who were with him on the holy mountain" (2 Pet. 1).

The majesty of the Word should not be understood to apply to the untransfigured flesh of Jesus Christ, in which the scorn and poverty of the cross led to death. Rather, it refers to the time after his resurrection and ascension, when his body entered glory and majesty. It was transfigured with the brilliance of the divine Word which dwells in his body. Now he has equality with God. Once he was transfigured in his mortal flesh; how glorious his immortal flesh must be! Now for all time the One who is lord of our understanding declares the hidden story of his transfiguration on the mount to be part of his transfigured, immortal flesh for all time. According to Heb. 1, the whole person of Christ is the glory of God, the image of God's invisible being. His whole humanity, outwardly in the flesh and inwardly in the spirit, is Godhead.

In its divinity, his human body now has God's eyes and face and comeliness in fullness, without blemish. . . . From Rev. 3 and other passages we see that Christ can know all things. He can act through the Holy Spirit as God the Father worked from the beginning of creation through the Holy Spirit. The Spirit has become the Son's arm and finger.[89] Nevertheless, he never had to leave heaven, which Scripture describes as grand and unique. Even today, according to his divine nature, the Lord Jesus Christ does not need to leave it in order to work his will, which he does everywhere. How much less does he leave heaven in his human nature, his transfigured body and blood. According to his human nature, he can't be everywhere – only one place at a time.

As we understand Schwenckfeld's view in several of his articles, *Christ's transfigured flesh and blood, like his divine nature, is everywhere, even in the true food and drink of the Lord's Supper.* On the mountain he was transfigured in his mortality, yet in his flesh and blood he couldn't be at more than one place. Ponder this: even now that his human, mortal nature has been transfigured, he can be in only one place.[90] Even while he was on earth he did his works where he was not present in body, for example, he healed the centurion's servant in absentia (Matt. 8). How much more in his glory and divinity can he work through his divine nature – eyes, fingers, Spirit, power – though his body is absent. Similarly, he is now able to do the work of his body, flesh, and blood even as he did on earth when he was not bodily present. [L. 497/*10-11*; *23*-498/*30*] . . .

. . . Earlier we discussed the two natures of Christ. Unless he wants to suspend or deny all of Holy Scripture, Schwenckfeld will have to confess this truth. Our question is, how can Christ's human nature be distinguished from his divine nature, granting that his two natures are united. Is it nothing more than terminology? Or do their characteristics and "graspability" need to be distinguished? . . . Otherwise, wouldn't their united and single will be deprived of something because no one has ever seen God, except for the Son of the Father, who is from the Father, he has seen him (John 6; 1 Tim. 6)?[91] All eyes will see the Son of Man but in his future glorified body (Rev.1; Matt. 24; Mark 14; Luke 13, 21). This will be in his human nature which is now caught up in his divinity. Yet it is the same humanity people saw after his bodily resurrection (Matt. 24; Mark 16; Luke 14; Acts 1; 1 Cor. 15). After his suffering, Christ let himself be seen alive for forty days, while he ate and drank with the apostles (Luke 24; Acts 10). Even after his ascension Stephen saw him sitting at the right hand of God in heaven (Acts 7). The human nature of Christ after the resurrection lost none of its properties; through the transfiguration it was established in a perpetual way. It is not only a matter of Christ, the Risen One, a transfigured human being now living in heaven, according to the Scriptures. Rather, God himself indwells the exalted (*veclerten*) humanity and body of Jesus Christ in fullness, as if in a physical place (Col. 2). God indwells all creatures in the humanity of Christ, in their bodies, natures, and distinctions – not in a single spatial location but in the humanity and body of Christ.[92] The exalted humanity of Christ, with its nature and distinctives, is henceforth not located in one place; it will never, ever, be displaced from the transfiguration and heavenly being it received. It sits at the right hand of God in power and glory. Schwenckfeld confesses this kind of humanity in his little discourse on Christ, when he says *"Christ is one person but has two natures; one Christ but two ways of being."*[93]

This transfigured person and spiritual body of Christ with his bodily humanity is the temple in which God lives because the corporeality of Christ has become part of God. It is the altar on which all holy sacrifices are offered to God's pleasure. It is the incense burner through which the incense is set alight – the prayer, thanksgiving, and praise in which all the saints arise in a sweet smell! It is the throne of grace by means of which God is gracious to people through himself. The embodied Christ is the eternal high priest who offers himself up for the people and through whom eternal redemption has been found.

This Christ, in his transfigured human nature, has the distinction of not being able to be at more than one place at one time. Even so, he is God through and through, transfigured in God, in whom God is all in all, localized or not. Both natures remain united and undivided forever, yet each nature has its unconfined (*ungenommen*) distinctives. If anyone should bind the divine nature of Jesus Christ to one place or time contrary to its own character and Holy Scripture, other than what we have set forth above, the divine nature of Christ would be denied. Again, if you attribute many locations to the humanity or the body of Christ (as Schwenckfeld does in his booklet) you deny the human manner, character, and nature of Christ. For it is of the essence of human nature that you can only be in one place at one time; it is of the essence of divine nature that it may be everywhere at the same time – to say nothing of its elegant dwelling in heaven and in the person and body of Christ.[94] Schwenckfeld confesses the two natures in and of Christ, but does he confess each with its individual character? If not, it wouldn't be two but one, what he subscribes to in his booklet notwithstanding. Otherwise, he would have to follow the error that Christ's human nature dissolved in his divine nature. Or perhaps he discarded it, or the Word of God had a human nature before his incarnation, or the Eternal Word incarnated itself without taking on Mary's created and creaturely flesh and blood. As hard as it is to believe, some mistaken people have held to such gross error. . . .

Schwenckfeld claims in his booklet that Jesus Christ, as a human being, discarded all the earthly, natural life in his body and flesh through his death, resurrection, and transfiguration, such that he no longer needs an earthly location, as he once did. Understand, "earthly" manner, that is, severed from all circumscription and placement in this old, earthly being. On the contrary, the Lord has taken a divine, heavenly, glorious, almighty essence upon himself, in which he now reigns in the heavenly realm with and in God. There he works for our salvation.[95] But he has a dwelling place – albeit in a heavenly essence and order – up in heaven whither he was taken after his resurrection and where he will be until the last judgement, according to Gospel Scripture and the articles of our common faith.[96]

For that reason, it's not possible according to our common faith, for him to be in another place or many places in his transfigured body, flesh, and blood – to say nothing of his being able to be in believers' hearts. He has this ubiquitous presence according to his divine nature as true, almighty God, divinely and spiritually with divine eyes, arms, and fingers, as we mentioned above. He is everywhere in heaven, on earth, and under the earth. In every moment he sees and works with his divine eyes and arms what God the Father and the Word is, having made the human being Jesus Christ with his body, flesh, and blood his own. The eternal, almighty Word, as divinity, has put on flesh. As something that belonged to him, Christ carried his flesh up into glory and divinity. He lives in it and bears it in a transfigured manner as his possession. In the same way, the transfigured flesh of Christ is possessed of his divinity. So, Jesus Christ is true, almighty God according to both natures but in one person. Even though this is in a heavenly manner, he has no less of a human nature. The unity and indivisibility of both natures is immovable; he is one person in two undivided natures. Through this union the physicality of Christ with the Word is God: the fullness of the Godhead dwells in him bodily[97] because Christ's bodiliness is now a part of God.

In him God took on flesh and lived in it. Before Christ's death, resurrection, and transfiguration, the Godhead did not dwell in him in that form, though by Spirit and Word he was God. But after his resurrection and the transfiguring of his body and flesh, the Godhead is in him not only according to Word and Spirit – as Paul says in Col. 2 – but in fullness, i.e., bodily. Through his exaltation Christ's body and flesh entered divine clarity and became fully God. It's not that the divine nature in and of itself has a human bodiliness, because John 4 tells us that God is Spirit. It happens in the uniting of both natures, body and spirit, flesh and Word. By means of the transfiguration we can understand that God as Word became flesh, in, with, and through the flesh he took upon himself. Through his perfect indwelling he took on bodiliness and inhabited it fully. [L. 500/*5-502/28*]

## X. The Word of God

. . . The transfigured Lord, the human being Jesus Christ, is true God in, through, and with the Word, according to both of his united natures. Beyond that, there is a difference in the characteristics of either nature. Such a transfigured Lord, as the human being Jesus Christ, according to both natures one God living in heaven, speaks the Word through the Holy Spirit. His Word comes down from heaven into the inner ear of believing human hearts, as a living Word of God, which Word and Spirit are God and Christ himself (John 1, 8; 2 Cor. 3; Rev. 19).[98] All things were made through him (John 1). This creative action is also ascribed to the Holy Spirit, as in Psalm 33: "The heavens were made through the Word of God and all his hosts through the mouth of his Spirit." "The Spirit of the Lord made me," says Job 13, "and the breath of the Almighty gave me life." Therefore, God's Word and Spirit are one in the divine power of their working. Even Schwenckfeld confesses this in his Cathechism[99]: *"God's Word is the wisdom of the Father, the Spirit of life, the arm of the right hand of God, God Christ the Lord. As even Christ says, 'My words are spirit and life '"* (John 6).

Still today, the Lord Jesus Christ, through the Holy Spirit, is at work in baptism (Matt. 3; Mk. 1; Luke 3) and the new birth (John 3), in assuring us that we are children of God (Rom. 8), and bringing us to life (John 6). He comforts, recalls, and teaches, leading us into all truth (John 14-17) and in uttering it (Acts 1, 2; 2 Pet. 1; Matt. 10; 1 Cor. 12; Rom. 10). Likewise, the Word of God as word of truth accomplishes the new birth, which comes from God (1 Pet. 1; Jas. 1). God's Word and Spirit work together. They proceed from the undivided, the one Jesus Christ – as they proceeded from the Father before the incarnation of the Word to things (*dingen*) in need. Today the Spirit and the Word proceed from the Son Jesus Christ to the actions which need doing today, ceaselessly, yet without his forsaking heaven with his body, flesh, and blood. Holy Scripture confines him to the place where he lives *(darinnen ine h. Schrift yetzt wonende umbschreibt!).* That is easier to grasp by faith when we see the clear witness of Holy Scripture against Schwenckfeld's opinion and undertaking. Several times his writings about the Lord in heaven arise out of his own spirit and are thick with concealment and unclarity.

As we have described it, God's Word and Spirit proceed from the transfigured Jesus Christ, who lives in heaven. We did this so people could see and recognize that the Lord works all things today through the Word and the Spirit who proceed from him. Before his incarnation the Father worked in this way, so there is no need for him to descend in his bodiliness until the day of judgement.[100]

If the transfigured flesh, body, and blood of Christ – that is, Christ in his human nature – is to be everywhere that he is according to his divine nature, he would need a human body as vast as his divine body. He would need to extend above and under heaven and earth. In sum, he would need to be where his divinity in his divine nature is, filling heaven and earth. Each of his members would need to have such a body and get around as Christ does. But they wouldn't be able to get anywhere because he would already be there. In that case, the Scriptures which speak of a bodily future would be erroneous, including the one which says that, after their resurrection, believers will be whisked toward the Lord in the air. But if they already possessed his likeness and were everywhere, they would already have been with him in the air.[101]

... Earlier we said that Schwenckfeld does not write correctly about the Word of God in his Catechism.[102] He comes out against the spoken words of those who want "this is my body" to mean that the body is in the bread. [He writes:] *"They don't deliberately err, but it is pertinent to say that they put more attention on what kind of word it is to which the Scriptures give such honour and power. Is this word the Scriptures themselves or the outwardly preached word, in an audible voice, taken from Scripture? Or, is it not rather much more a higher, namely, a natural (sic) and almighty word, which is spirit and life – indeed, is God himself? Actually, the Holy Scriptures are a living, essential word of God and not a written repetition of another's words or the letter of divine power. Scripture and the outwardly preached word point and attest to this alone."*

Schwenckfeld continues,[103] *"There are two kinds of words of God, as we commonly speak of them, namely, an inward, eternal word of the Spirit, and an outward, transitory word of Scripture or the letter. The outward word stands in the order of earthly things, of perishable essences; it is only a witness of the inner word, even if it is needed in spiritual and divine actions in the service of Christ. But according to its nature and substance it is not spirit or life but something written, sounded, or voiced. In itself it is flesh – without grace – a fleeting and dead creature on earth."*

We answer what Schwenckfeld says in this way: Wouldn't it be fitting to pay more attention to the nature of this word to which the Scriptures attribute so much glory and power, whether it be Scripture itself or the outwardly preached word whose sound and voice are taken from Scripture? Schwenckfeld should know that the invisible, spiritual content and meaning of Holy Scripture and the outwardly preached word is the very word which Scripture, as we shall show, gives glory and power as God's natural, almighty word. It is spirit and life, yes, God himself. It is not a visible, perishing book of paper and ink; it is the eternal, living, essential word of God. The Scriptures and outward preaching don't only witness to it – as Schwenckfeld says – but they themselves are that word, through their visible, spiritual sense,[104] proceeding from God and the Holy Spirit as spirit and life. They come from [the] God Christ, and the Holy Spirit into the heart through faith.[105] Since it is Christ in us, it is the very Word to which the Scriptures give honour and might, through whom all things were made (John 1; Col. 1). Just as such a Word of God dwells in the heart of the believer, so it is also, besides that, in outward understanding a single, undivided essence, not two but a single Word of God. Scripture and sermon are a co-witness, i.e., similar additional witnesses which concur with the inner, single Word of God. [L. 516/*22*-518/*31*] . . .

. . . Schwenckfeld calls a written, repeated word a perishing word – not spirit and life but a script, a sound, a voice. It is mere flesh, a transitory creature on earth. But we say that it is and becomes an expressed word from God and Jesus Christ through the Holy Spirit, a single word of address with the inwardly impressed word. It comes from God and Christ because through the Holy Spirit it is a word not only *into* the heart but spoken and proclaimed *from* the heart of believers.[106] [L. 519/*36-47*] . . .

. . . Jeremiah called Baruch the son of Nerie to write down all the speeches of the Lord which came from the mouth of Jeremiah. Baruch did his best to carry out Jeremiah's request: he read from the book of the Lord's speeches in the Lord's house. Listen to him: "Thus says the Lord God of Israel, Diligently write down all the conversations I have had with you in a book" (Jer. 30). Remember Exodus 32, "Moses turned and descended from the mountain. He had two tablets of witness in his hand; they were inscribed on both sides and were God's testimony." Their script was God's script engraved. We also claim that the Holy Spirit wrote the Gospel and apostolic Scriptures through the hand of the evangelists and apostles. Therefore, they are the writing of God or the Holy Spirit. For those reasons, the speeches and words of God and the Holy Spirit composed in Scripture are praised and declared to be holy (2 Tim. 3; Rom. 1). Yes, they are called the writing of God (Isa. 34).

On this basis the Lord spoke to the Jews. "The Father who has sent me has borne witness to me: you have neither heard his voice nor seen his form. His word does not live within you, because you do not believe the one whom he has sent. You look for me in the Scripture for you think you have life in it. It bears witness to me yet you do not want to come to me, that you might have life" (John 5). The Lord states that the Scripture which witnesses to him and his salvation, is life. Similarly, in John 6 he talks about his bodily spoken words as words of salvation,[107] saying, "The words which I spoke are spirit and life, but some among you do not believe it." See, here he compares the physical or outward sermon and Holy Scripture: both sound forth his salvation. Such preaching and the written word of God are one. One of them is spirit and life as much as the other, namely, through faith in the heart, that is, through the gift and inspiration of God the Holy Spirit. But without faith it is naught, even though it remains God's spoken and written word.[108] [L. 521/*1-33*] . . .

. . . Schwenckfeld writes, "*I say that God's word is an eternally living word which descends from the mouth of God into the believing soul without creaturely or instrumental means. It is the wisdom of the Father, of the Spirit and life, the arm of the one who sits at the right hand of the Father, God Christ, the Lord.*"[109]

We reply: Here he is speaking blatantly and coarsely against apostolic writing because the Holy Spirit as an inspirer of the word, yes, the word himself, will not be received without the outward means of preaching about faith (Gal. 3; Eph. 1). . . . It comes about through the outward apostolic office and ministry of the Spirit. Paul states that this office gives the Spirit; he calls himself and his fellow-apostles ministers of the Spirit (2 Cor. 3; Phil. 3). He also says that the enlightenment brought about by the knowledge of the glory of God in the face of Jesus Christ comes about through him and other apostles (2 Cor. 4). The apostles or ministers of the Spirit are creaturely human instruments, the armour of God (Acts 9; 2 Cor. 5; 1 Cor. 3). For God does his work in people through them (Matt. 10; Acts 15, 19; Rom. 15; 2 Cor. 2, 5). So Paul says to the Corinthians, "I have brought you to birth through Christ Jesus in the Gospel" (1 Cor. 14[:?]). Therefore, Schwenckfeld is wrong to claim that the word or Holy Spirit descends into the believing soul from the mouth of God without the medium of creatures or instruments. In his *Judgement*, which is wrong from start to finish, he has the habit of overthrowing outward things which God and Christ the Lord instituted (such as teaching, preaching, baptism,

Lord's Supper, and Scripture) as a means for people to come to inner reality. . . . What devices the devil desires to subvert people! He knows how to succeed and he knows how his deeds will hurt people. God had a purpose: he didn't ordain his means in vain. But to rob God of his purpose, the enemy is at work talking people out of God's means and trying to abolish them.

Schwenckfeld continues, *"The water of the word of God which Jesus Christ has in mind is also spoken about in Ephesians 5 by Paul. 'Christ loved the church and offered himself up for it in order to sanctify it. He purified it through the water bath of the water through the word.' This is not outward baptismal water, as some falsely interpret it; this is the Holy Spirit."*[110] Here Schwenckfeld severs the unity of baptism into parts, the outward from the inward, as he does in the first part of his false *Judgement*. We hold that this quotation about the water bath in the word concerns itself with a single, undivided baptism, as he writes in Eph. 4, "one Lord, one faith, one baptism." This baptism belongs together in harmony; the outward witnesses with the inward. We have already written above concerning baptism and the water bath. . . Just as the inward and the outward are together in the Lord's Supper, so the inner and outer spoken word minister together and are one. [L. 529/35-530/9] . . .

## XI. More Christology

. . . In Schwenckfeld's booklet "On Knowing Christ" we read the following: *"Therefore, Christ Jesus had to put away all this creaturely essence, all this earthly life bound to the flesh and take upon himself a divine, heavenly, glorious essence if he wanted to beget many children and bring them to heavenly glory (Heb. 1). The writers wanted to attest to the fact that Christ is no longer with us in a human, bodily manner but only spiritually, in a way that is incomprehensible to reason. Yet he remains present to us; he remains truly divine and human."* And again, *"Through death the Lord Jesus has put off his whole creaturely essence and life; even in his humanity he has become lord of all creatures in heaven and on earth."*[111]

In the above citations Schwenckfeld attests clearly that the flesh of Christ was not creaturely before his death.[112] Therefore, it could not be called "a new creature" after his resurrection since it never was one before his death. The flesh that died with Christ was also raised with him; it was restored and transfigured and glorified – it and none other. It has a relationship with the mortal flesh of all other Christians; through Christ it is and will be restored and be a new creature in the sense of the text which was quoted. Otherwise, it would follow that God did not take our old, mortal flesh as the medium of restoration. It means that the same flesh was not brought to life for everlasting glory or suffering but that God created a new and different flesh. That is a vast, terrible, and destructive error. [L. 532/35-533/9] . . .

. . . It is no small comfort and hope to the human race that human flesh as part of Christ's humanity now sits at the right hand of God in heavenly glory. Christ's humanity is our mediator between God and humanity, our high priest and intercessor. Christ reigns; he has become very God of very God (*gott in und durch gott worden*). Peter writes that God has given him glory, so that you might believe and have hope in God (1 Pet. 1[:21], not verbatim). It is written, "He had to be made like his brothers in every respect, so that he might become a merciful and faithful high priest before God to reconcile the sins of the people. Because he himself has suffered and been tempted, he is able to help those who are tempted" (Heb. 2[:17-18]). Hear the words in Heb. 5, "We do not have a high priest who is unable to sympathize with our weakness."[113]

Therefore, Schwenckfeld is right when he says, "*We should gladly honour him who is the mediator between God and humanity. As he had said, he participates autonomously and naturally in both parties between whom he mediates. Augustine writes that Christ needed to have what would make him equal to God and to humanity. For that reason he is called Deus Homo, 'God-man,' by Augustine and other of the fathers.*"[114]

This is what Schwenckfeld and Augustine say! The fact that Jesus Christ is part of our flesh gives birth to hope, faithfulness, mediation, and intercession with God. For that reason we say, if his flesh were not our flesh, we would have but little comfort and hope. [L. 536/30-537/5] . . .

. . . We gladly admit that the origin and advent of Christ's humanity comes from God's Word and Holy Spirit, thus not from God in the sense in which he created the first Adam. Romans 5 presents a picture of the other Adam, Christ, in his humanity. For the first Adam was carved out of the already created but still lifeless earth without sin according to the human spirit, as an inner being. He was not filled with God himself but breathed into by God's breath. . . . But Jesus Christ the human being, the essential Adam, according to the flesh is not divine by nature but from the Spirit.[115] He was carved out of the earth of the living (Isa. 53) – born (Heb. 3) and prepared (Heb. 10[:5]). As a mortal, he proceeded from the living womb of

Mary. In the Spirit, as an inner being, he was not merely breathed into by divine breath but – from his birth on – was breathed into as the Word, the Holy Spirit, even God himself. He was not created or made, nor was he of human flesh, blood, and creatureliness. He was without beginning and from eternity the everlasting God and Spirit, but within time he was made flesh (John 1). Please understand, he was not newly created but was born of pre-created (*vorgeschoepften*) flesh of human generation in the body of Mary. And, as the first, figurative Adam had no father in his birth other than God alone and lifeless earth as his mother, from which God made him according to the flesh, so also the human Christ as the essential Adam had no other father than God alone and the earth of the living, that is, human, creaturely generation in his birth and incarnation. He came to the tribe of Judah and to the body of Mary, his mother. From her God carved out Jesus' flesh, prepared through his holy and divine activity (Heb. 3:10).[116] Schwenckfeld confesses from Rev. 5 that Jesus Christ is from the tribe of Judah and the root of David.[117]

In this and no other way did the origin and advent of the human being Christ happen. He was born out of God and the Holy Spirit and out of a remarkable act of God the Father, from his nature and essence, and from the Virgin Mary, full of grace and blessing under the sway of the Holy Spirit. He is not under the sentence which applies to Adam's children; rather, this person Jesus Christ was conceived and born without sin through a novel, divine action. It was not according to the will or working of the flesh or a man's or woman's desire for offspring (*erblichen begierd*). No, the chaste virgin, Mary, spoke, "How can this be, since I do not know a man?" (Luke 1). And so it was that she stood pure, empty, and free, prepared for this holy incarnation of Jesus Christ through the encroachment, that is, the unique favour of God.

This is the difference between Christ's creaturely flesh and ours: it was not born *as* ours is, although it was born *from* and *of* our flesh. But as to our birth, from the first moment we are under the sentence of bodily death through Adam's sin; that is our inheritance. It follows, then, in approaching the knowledge of good and evil, that we may sin and receive eternal death.

From birth onward he was free because of his remarkable, supernatural conception and birth. According to the Spirit he was God, yes, life itself. Because of that he had no desire to sin and no need to die eternally. Every sin happens through the perversion of the human spirit by the devil's doing. The plot is decided and conceived within us (Matt. 15; Mark 7). Christ was and is the very sinlessness and changelessness of God. He neither sinned nor suffered perversion nor moved anyone to sin but was a shield against it. None of this had any place in Christ's spirit. Because of his holy flesh and his pure, immaculate conception and birth, there was no deceit, lust, evil inclination, or inherited remnants from Adam's fall in him. So much holier and purer is his natural flesh than ours: he bears God himself and not merely God's breath, as in our case. He is divine; flesh and blood of the Word and the Spirit (Acts 20[118]). Even so, it follows that he is also a creature of the generation of mortal human beings.

For all the reasons listed we conclude that the Lord Jesus Christ never sinned; he was unable to do so (1 Pet. 2; Isa. 53). He is separated from sinners (Heb. 7 [:26-28]); in John 8 no one was able to point out his sins. Neither the prince of this world nor anyone else found sin in him (John 14). Because of that, Christ did not have to die; he did so out of free love (John 10). Because he was not born as we were, death and its pangs could not hold him, nor could his soul be abandoned to hell. His flesh did not see corruption (Acts 2:13),[119] as was the case with Adam's other children. He didn't have to die, but he wanted to die; therefore, he participated in our mortal flesh and blood according to the Scriptures (Heb. 2). Similarly, he was born of Mary but without remnants of Adam's inheritance, so that he could take our human weakness upon himself (Isa. 53; Matt. 8, 2; 2 Cor. 13).[120] In human weakness he triumphed over the world and its powers. This is the Lion from the tribe of Judah, the root of David, he and none other (Rev. 3:5; John 16).[121] Whoever receives his flesh as an inheritance of the fall – as all human beings other than Jesus do – must die within the bounds of time, whether one wants to or not. Thus, the Word or God (sic), as life itself, took on flesh at his own initiative and came down from heaven. He did not take on our flesh or he would not have wanted to die: death cannot come from life. God, as life itself, cannot die; he alone has immortality (1 Tim. 6). If that were the case, the Scripture would be untrue when it states that he participated in our flesh and blood – without contradicting what is creaturely – in order to take away the might of him, who has the power of death, the devil, by dying (Heb. 2). [L. 541/*28*-543/ *27*] . . .

. . . A new beginning  has come in Jesus Christ, but it does not remove creatureliness from Christ or those who belong to him; it is not lost but renewed within the temporal order through the new birth. In the eternal order there is a bodily resurrection and transfiguration so that mortal flesh arises physically – but in incorruptable, immortal, spiritual form – into glory. All flesh which dies in Christ, and none other, will arise in him and be led into glory, even as Job attests: "In the end he will awaken me from the earth. After that I will be enclosed in my skin; in my flesh I shall see God. I shall see him and my eyes shall behold him" (Job 19).[122] [L. 545/*31-43*] . . .

. . . God made the body of woman, meaning Eve, out of man, out of Adam's body, flesh, and bone, as Genesis 2 states. He also made a man, the one man Jesus Christ, out of a woman, the one woman the Virgin Mary – out of her body, blood, and bone, though not without a distinctive action, as is written in Matt. 1 and Luke 1. We write this so that no one can say: God is unable to make a woman from a man's body, or in contrast, a man's body out of woman's. There is a general order of creation which testifies to the fact that a female is born from a male and a male from a female, in that often the daughter resembles the father and the son the mother in shape, form, and voice. [L. 547/*1-13*] . . .

. . . The ancient theologians teach that the humanity of Christ was creaturely. Whatever form and reason there was to their argument, it goes against Schwenckfeld's teaching, who negates any creatureliness in Christ. In our judgement, the ancients taught the creatureliness of Christ just as we do, drawing it from the foundation and witness of Scripture. [L. 547/*38-43*] . . .

. . . Schwenckfeld cites Ambrose: "*After the resurrection Christ was God through and through*[123]: *we no longer know Christ according to the flesh. We should note that even though Ambrose had compelling reasons to state that the flesh of Christ was created (because of heretics), he also noted the entire mystery of the incarnation. But with it he did not wish to abrogate the glory of Christ at all, but to claim him to be the natural Son of God even in his humanity and to bestow on him the honourable status of the other person in the Godhead at the right hand of the Father. His flesh is to be adored; Christ is God according to his humanity.*"

The intention of our position and our description of the mystery of Christ's incarnation is not to take anything away from Christ's glory. We hold him to be the natural Son of God according to his humanity. . . . We are to understand his created flesh as a precreated being, participating in the creaturely flesh of Mary. We agree with Schwenckfeld and include the incarnate one in the honourable status of the other person in the Godhead at the right hand of the Father. Christ is God according to his humanity; his transfigured, divinized, and glorified flesh is to be adored. We also recognize that Ambrose wrote according to the knowledge of the heart and not only because of heresy or other movements. He did not go against his heart knowledge or he would have been false, deceptive, and unjust. We too confess the creatureliness of Christ because of the truth in our heart: we adore Christ. We deify the glorified humanity of Christ as very God, God in God, as is right. [L. 548/5-35] . . .

. . . We will not concern ourselves with the witness of the Holy Trinity except to confess one person of the Word and his flesh. This agrees with the first epistle of St. John, chapter 5, when [John] speaks about Christ after his ascension and transfiguration. "There are three who give witness in heaven: the Father, the Word, and the Holy Spirit, and the three have one ministry."[124] That is the Holy Trinity. The glorified and divinized flesh of Christ, ascended to heaven, is part of the Word. . . . Otherwise John would have to say, "There are four who give witness in heaven: the Father, the Word, the flesh of Christ, and the Holy Spirit." The human flesh of Christ is included in the Holy Trinity as part of a single Godhead, to be worshiped with the Word as God, because it is neither alongside nor outside of God but equally one with God. [L. 550/34-47] . . .

. . . The human flesh and blood and bone of Christ, as described, shares equality in the Holy Trinity in and with the Word. He is a life-giving human being through the abundant flowing of the oil of joy (which he possesses), that is, the anointing of the holy, quickening Spirit. Therefore, all true believers become members of his body through the life-giving humanity of Christ through the anointing of the Holy Spirit. . . . They are anointed as children of God, Christ, and the Holy Spirit, and born as new creatures, so that in their creaturely flesh and bone they conform to his creaturely yet all-holy divine flesh and bone (Rom. 8). Made from his flesh, Christ and his church are two who have become one flesh, spiritually speaking, as Paul says in Eph. 5. We have this form not only by being born of the flesh and bone of Christ but, as Schwenckfeld says, *"we are (as Paul says) members of his body, flesh of his flesh and bone of his bone."*[125] He doesn't say "born," though it's not wrong to stick to that little word because a spiritual birth is at issue: all grace comes from the humanity of Christ. Without it we could not come to God or become God's children.

As we have said, Christ and Christians are a single flesh through spiritual birth, which the Lord, the human being Jesus Christ as God, works in us. Therefore, the flesh of Christians is no longer a godless, impure flesh because it stands in the unity of faith. According to 2 Cor. 7, Eph. 5, and Heb. 10 we are purified from our stain. Our sinful body is crucified, we have put off the flesh and its works. We have died through the Spirit, so we no longer live according to the sinful flesh but according to the Spirit. We do not follow fleshly desires but keep ourselves from them (Rom. 6, 8, 13; Gal. 5, 6; 1 Thess. 4; 1 Pet. 2). If the believer forsakes the simplicity of faith, then he follows not the Christian flesh but godless flesh and stains the sanctified flesh of Christ in him (Jude 1). . . . The flesh of believers is of one flesh with Christ. He does not hate his own flesh (Eph. 5)!

There is a distinction in Scripture concerning the word "flesh." There are two kinds of human flesh. First, there is a pure one which has died to sin and been divinized. Second, there is the impure one. Both are God's creatures with the following distinction. Impure flesh cannot inherit the kingdom of God. Whoever puts on impure flesh is called carnally minded and lives according to, and is born from, the will of the flesh. In their pure flesh Christians no longer know anyone according to carnal flesh. Even fallen flesh is a creature of God but only aside from its fallenness. The fall was not created by God. . . Schwenckfeld errs in his marginal note, "*A pure person without God is a creaturely, adamic person.*"[126] We say that a pure person without God is a godless and fallen one; he does not bear a likeness to Adam. Before the fall he was a good and upright creature. Even godless people are creatures but with the difference of sin and the fall. But all creatures of God were created good (Gen. 2; 1 Tim. 4).[127] [L. 552/*23*-553/*28*] . . .

. . . In this present age God's word makes us spiritual and heavenly through a new birth in our inward and hidden person (Eph. 3; 1 Pet. 3). Through the Holy Spirit we are assured in our inward person that we are children of God (Rom. 8) and are at one with God. Through God's constancy his Spirit and ours may be called one spirit, according to Paul in 1 Cor. 6. Born of the Spirit, we are called spirit (John 3) and so, even in this age, we are called spiritual beings. We resist the sinful work of the flesh through the Holy Spirit and crucify our flesh with its lusts. Even within this present age we are called spiritual beings (1 Cor. 2; Gal. 6; Rom. 8). But it doesn't follow that our bodies are also spiritual in this age, as they will be after the bodily resurrection. Now they are earthly and have need of earthly places, dwellings, order, food, drink, and conversation.[128] As the proverb puts it, in this age the human spirit does not cry out until we have crossed the stream after the triumph of resurrection. That is so because here in this life our human spirit can still sin, fall, and be misled. The flesh itself could not be misled, were it not for our spirit and its distortion. Instead of silencing the human spirit we silence the flesh (*Und in disem gefar stat hie in zeit der menschlich geist, zu schweigen das fleisch*). Thus Paul says, "Whoever thinks he is standing should look out, lest he fall" (1 Cor. 10).

After the bodily resurrection the bodies of believers will become spiritual and their human spirit, that is, the hidden person, will indisputably take on the likeness of the heavenly humanity of Christ.[129] . . . Then, through the transfiguring might of God they will have the power to be visible or invisible. . . . In this age their inner person is hidden but their untransfigured flesh does not now endow them with invisibility. That comes only with the resurrection of the body and its spiritual possibilities, because a natural body will give way to a supernatural one of invisible Gospel luminosity. . . . How can we take the measure of the Scriptures which describe the future glory of true believers, beholding the radiant countenance of Christ's transfigured humanity? . . . Just as in his transfigured humanity the Lord became a life-giving spirit,[130] in his flesh he became a life-giving Word. Through his divine anointing he became a life-giving spirit without annulling his flesh. [L. *557/32-558/31*] . . .

. . . We have said enough about creatures! In closing let us say that the flesh of Christ together with the Word is now God. It is there that all sinners find refuge. Without it nobody would be saved or come to the eternal God. In his great love and mercy to our ruined race, God sent his eternal Son who took upon himself our race's flesh – yet without sin. Thereby he became the potentate and mediator between God and humanity for our salvation. Whoever would be saved must seek salvation at the throne of the human Christ's grace. . . . Whoever has the man Jesus, has the Father also; whoever does not have Jesus' favour, does not have the Father's either. That is the gist of the matter.[131] [L. *558/48-559/11*] . . .

## XII. More on the Lord's Supper

The first reference in our previous testimony was to Oecolampadius's and Zwingli's understanding of the words "this is my body."[132] Their opinion is that those words were spoken figuratively and must be understood figuratively. They should be understood to say, "this bread signifies my body or is a mental sign (*denkzaichen*) of my body." This was our response: "With reference to the words, 'this is my body,' and with reference to bread and wine, and how they are to be understood, we can only interpret them in a figurative manner; that is, we must interpret them, not as they were spoken *in ordinary speech even though the Scriptures use them in a commonsensical way*.[133] We stand by these words and by our general understanding of the Lord's words. "*As Christ says*, 'This is my body which is given for you' can naturally and concretely be interpreted to mean his actual body, which sat at the table and which was also betrayed and truly given for us. But the bread and the wine must be understood figuratively to mean the bread we break and the wine we drink, during which we are to remember the body and blood of Christ and to remember that Christ's body was given for us and his blood was shed for us."

This is our complete understanding of the words of Christ.[134] If Schwenckfeld had wanted to judge justly, he would not have taken our words about figures in isolation but taken what follows in the condensation of our views on essence and figure. But he makes a cheap accusation based only on our first thoughts, as if we don't take the words of Christ – when he talks about his self with the little word "is" (this *is* my body) – to be spirit, life, and eternal truth. As if we take it to be only a figure or a picture! . . . The Lord spoke in proverbs, parables, and the like; they are spirit and life if received in divine wisdom. To that end they are judged by all true believers as spirit and life. In the words of our testimony you can see clearly that we take neither the Lord's word nor the Lord himself as a figure but as truth and essence. We restrict figurative language to bread and wine to the extent that the words "this is my body" concern bread and wine and are to be taken as such. To that extent we take them metaphorically, that is, on another level of understanding than they naturally express. But in their natural expression we understand them not as figures but as essence. They refer to his real body, which entered death on our behalf, which we eat and drink as we have written.[135] How then can Schwenckfeld accuse us of an injustice? Is he saying that we don't know what we're doing, as if we have two contradictory understandings, trying to mix together the natural and the figurative? Does he think that the Lord can't speak in twofold meanings?

If he wants to judge by the standard of love, Schwenckfeld should fairly consider that before the Lord's death he spoke in proverbs and parables (Matt. 13; John 16). His understanding was on two levels, first through a parable, and following that he penetrated to the essence which was signified by the parable. The meanings are not adverse to each other but are composed of a single, right understanding. The Lord is not twofold in his speech, because the two levels serve each other. It's not all black and white, as Schwenckfeld claims in his marginal comment! Together a single colour emerges with a single meaning. Schwenckfeld's conclusion simply doesn't follow. If Christ spoke the words "this is my body" with reference to his body seated at the table, could he not also have been making reference to the bread and wine?

Further, Schwenckfeld should consider his unceremonious references to the word of God... He mentions the outwardly spoken words of Christ, "this is my body," and then denies that outwardly spoken words of Christ are spirit and life. He goes on: *such outwardly spoken words of Christ belong in the order of earthly things, of this passing reality. Its nature is not spirit and life but flesh and frailty. ...*

Listen to Schwenckfeld. *"Both interpretations are wrong. The Lord did not say 'my body is sitting right here' but he also didn't say 'this bread signifies my body.'"* The words of institution should not be understood by means of such empty, fruitless talk. But he continues: *"After the breaking and eating of bread, Christ said 'this is my body' to show through the parable of broken and eaten bread what was the nature and character of his body and that he was the true food. He said the same of the blood."*

Earlier Schwenckfeld denied that the bread didn't refer to Christ's body. Here he turns it around and claims it as a parable. In sum, you can see what he's after throughout the booklet. We say that through the parable of the broken and eaten bread Christ signifies what kind of body he has and that he is the true food of our souls. ... The same is true of the blood. ... [L. 559/*46*-560/*37*]

Our meaning seems contradictory and wrong to Schwenckfeld. He understands the words of Christ, "this is my body," only in relation to his above-mentioned classification, as if Christ's transfigured body, flesh, and blood is everywhere – even present in the Lord's Supper. In that form it is eaten and drunk by all believers as the true food. The words "eat, this is my body" are to be understood only on this level. But the Gospel witness is clear that in his words and actions Christ dealt with two forms. First is the essence, given through his word and body. Thereafter comes a figurative physical eating through bread and wine. ... [L. 561/*41-49*]

*"If they want to know something basic concerning the Lord's Supper,"* writes Schwenckfeld, *"if they want to comply with its true use and right understanding, they must learn to understand the Lord's words according to the meaning in his heart. They should disregard arguments over words and casuistry. The Lord himself attested to the fact that these words are spirit and life; they are the object of faith. How can those who don't have a good grasp of them rightly know the manner of breaking bread and the act of remembrance believe rightly? Indeed, how can they have communion with Christ? They should diligently read the sixth chapter of John if they want to come closer to the truth. We will let what they go on to write concerning the setting up of the Christ's church prove its worth. In brief, they write that the church has an outward way of life, expressed in baptism, teaching, ban, the Supper of Christ, and a lifestyle of piety and truth. In the* Admonition *they write that the church is built up through baptism.*[136] *Let us hold to the witness of Holy Scripture concerning the church of Christ and the writings of Paul concerning its construction. If things were as they set them forth, then there hasn't been a church or Christians for more than a thousand years. That would be a terrifying thing to hear!"*

We confess with Schwenckfeld in a summary, like the one he pens above, that we write without falsifying things as he accuses us of doing. We write without arguments or casuistry. Is he saying that we should not enquire into or try to understand the Lord's word or spiritual food in the Lord's Supper? He asserts this in [one place]. We say, whoever wants to celebrate the memory of the Lord rightly must do so with understanding and knowledge of his word. Let us grant Schwenckfeld that he has rightly understood the words of the Lord, the manner of breaking bread, and the memorial. Let us assume that he is not wrong in his opinion concerning the transfigured flesh and blood of Christ, that it is bodily present in communion as food and drink in all believing hearts.[137] But then he resists what we have clearly written [earlier]. From this error we sense that he wrongly takes the sixth chapter of John to be a parallel to the memorial the Lord ordained with creaturely bread and wine. This seems to be his interpretation in what he has written above. This does not tally! What the Lord said in John 6 concerning the true eating and drinking of his flesh and blood, we consider – without the misuse of creaturely things – to be spirit and life. It may not be taken as a parable of earthly food and drink, because the latter is only a memorial of the essential food and drink. The former is the eternal, essential meal, as we have attested to in our writing; it is not a memorial of the finished suffering of Christ. But the Lord instituted his Supper as a memorial of his finished and unrepeatable death, to be recalled and proclaimed.[138]

The flesh and blood of Christ, given up for us, is eternal food and drink for all of God's elect, as we have written. We believe that it was given up for us. In and after Christ's transfiguration his flesh and blood is not, as Schwenckfeld writes, the true food and drink of communion through a bodily presence in our hearts. The words of 1 Cor. 11 do not command us to "proclaim the Lord's transfigured presence in body and blood until he comes again" but to "proclaim his death until he comes again." Such proclamation would be a mockery. Schwenckfeld will have to understand these words according to the Lord's meaning and heart if he wants to know anything basic about the Lord's communion and its celebration. His erroneous meaning casts a shadow over the matter.

The sixth chapter of John concerns the eating of Christ's flesh and the drinking of his blood. In that chapter bread and wine are a parable and remembrance of the essential eating and drinking. Christ does not speak in John 6 of a remembrance; there is not a word of instruction to eat his flesh and blood as a memorial and thanksgiving, as he instituted in the Lord's Supper. His flesh and blood is not a memorial but that which one remembers. It is not a thanksgiving but he whom one thanks; not a proclamation but he whose death one proclaims. It is not a figurative food and drink like bread and wine or its use but the essential food and drink itself.[139] [L. 562/*15*-563/*42*]

### XIII. Conclusions

Schwenckfeld continues to accuse us that when we speak about the commissioning of the church we are writing other than the apostles did. In a note in the margin he describes our testimony about the church as untrue: *"it is to be commissioned and preserved through* true proclamation of the Gospel, correct baptism, [correct] communion, *and the ban and a walk of piety and truth. "*[140] We ask Schwenckfeld, through whom did the Lord command his church to be built? The apostles were commissioned to uphold the church through Gospel teaching, baptism, the Lord's Supper, the ban, and a lifestyle of piety and truth. Piety arises from the grace of Christ through faith in him (Rom. 5; 10; 13). . . . [L. 563/*43*-564/*6*]

... Schwenckfeld concludes that it would be a terrible thing if there had been no church or Christians for over a thousand years. ... If you don't remain in Christ's teaching you can't be a disciple of his, you have no God, in short, you can't be a Christian! Schwenckfeld despises the very teaching through which the church was commissioned and preserved. ... [L. 564/ *32-36*] That is terrible to hear, together with his false accusations and his false *Judgement*! He goes contrary to the apostolic teaching of Christ when he makes an erroneous proposal, namely that we should think of the water we sprinkle as a free sign of repentance and put a moratorium (*zufriden steen lassen*) on the Lord Christ's baptism. More remains to be said about his proposal and our answer. We confess that for over a thousand years, that is, since Christ's incarnation and ascension, Christ himself as well as his apostles taught about "the humanity of Christ." It consists of preaching, teaching, correct baptism, communion, ban, and Christian way of life. Because it was held to, there has always been a church and Christians. We proved this to be so in our citations of the ancients. The Christian church began after Christ's incarnation, death, resurrection, and ascension. That's more than a thousand years ago! The apostolic churches retained the whole teaching of Christ and his apostles: preaching, baptism, communion, ban, and Christian way of life. As it says, "They remained steadfast in the apostolic teaching, in community, in the breaking of bread, and in prayer" (Acts 2). All who follow such apostolic Christian churches in the teaching of Christ and the apostles are Christians and a Christian church. You can't be called "Christian" or a "Christian church" without that. [L. 564/*44*-565/ *20*]

Hear Schwenckfeld's proposal to the baptism brothers: "*I hope they come to a good-hearted conclusion about the* Judgement, *that is, about my judgement, on their booklet which they published for all to judge*," writes Schwenckfeld. "*I want to faithfully admonish all baptism brothers, teachers,*[141] *and listeners that they should look around carefully and not put their trust in baptism but in Jesus Christ the Lord. By his grace, they should come to a deeper knowledge of him and a godly life in order to rightly distinguish Christ's twofold commandments. Fundamental to everything is faith and a virtuous Christian life for those who want to be saved. Then there are others who hold to an outward church order, organization, and apostolic ministry. They should learn discernment and not let their consciences become entangled in outward things. My faithful admonition is to allow for a moratorium on all empty ceremonies through the Lord Jesus and his Holy Spirit.*" ... [L. 565/28-41]

... Schwenckfeld admonishes us to build on the foundation of Jesus Christ and to come ever nearer to him. But his desire is to lead us away from building on Christ as the right foundation and to deceive us. He advises us not to heed the baptism Christ commanded. He tells us to separate Christ's teachings about the inward and outward from each other. Don't have qualms of conscience, he says, about outward things, like outward church order, organization, ban, and apostolic service. Let there be a moratorium through the freedom we have in the Lord Jesus and the Holy Spirit. ... [L. 566/44-567/1] Even though the work of faith in Christ with baptism has two characteristics and effects – inward and outward, spiritual and bodily – yet together it is only one baptism and witness of truth (Eph. 4). For that which the Holy Spirit attests in the believing heart, that the believing heart attests with and through the outward person. This happens in obedience to the guidance of the Holy Spirit according to the human Christ's command through baptism and other acts. The truth lies in never separating or dividing the inward from the outward or the outward from the inward.[142] In our time the outward person is seldom obedient to the discipline of the Spirit. But there is a single person, spirit, soul, and body. Otherwise, it follows that the outward person would pursue the lusts of the flesh, that these would have no effect on the inward person, and that the outward person would be free from obedience to the Spirit. What a transaction of faith and obedience that would be!

Outward and inward need to be distinguished, but to divide them from each other according to Schwenckfeld's conclusion – as if we are not bound to the outward in matters of faith – is an open deception carried out against Christ's teaching, command, and institution, indeed, against the foundation of truth. Otherwise, it must follow that the obedience of faith is of no consequence to the outward person and to the human body. ... [L. 567/8-31] ... How could one live a blessed life and learn to know Christ (as Schwenckfeld says); how could one have faith in Christ, without preaching or teaching? Mark what the enemy has in mind: to give up the outward meeting together of Christians (which is part of church order). That would be against Paul's teaching which commends the meeting of Christians the more because the day of the Lord draws near (Heb. 10). This refers to the Lord's return. There is no middle time of postponement or cessation. In this very chapter Paul is addressing people who had ceased meeting together. This is what Schwenckfeld advocates. How, then, can one learn to know Christ and live a blessed life according to his teaching when one ceases to meet together to be edified and admonished? ...[143] [L. 567/*38-49*]

... To be sure, the inner person is free from all outward doing and letting be because we can't do either good or ill on our own anyway. All outward works, good or evil, originate in a good or evil spirit which takes outward expression. The life of a good inner person is hidden with Christ in God (Col. 3). The life of an evil inner person is hidden under seeming piety in the devil until the revelation of judgement. Through the obedience of faith, works of piety break forth in outward expression, done by human beings, revealing salvation. ... [L. 568/*11-21*]

... If we have been made holy through faith in Jesus Christ (which we hope) and if the Spirit of grace has assured our spirit, then we are believers in Jesus Christ and, therefore, his members, his body, his church. It alone carries out the great transaction of Christ, which he commands us to act out in baptism, communion, and other celebrations. These we do together with others. On the basis of our souls' salvation we are obedient: we know that we are debtors. Our obedience comes not from doing things right in our own strength; we do them through the Lord Jesus Christ, who lives in us (Gal. 2), who is all in all to true believers (Col. 3). Without him we would be too weak, too unwise, too unlearned to be his agents. In us he is strength enough, our power and wisdom (1 Cor. 1). Through his Holy Spirit he teaches and leads us into all truth to the kingdom of heaven. Our intention is to live out what we have confessed, grounded in the truth and witness of Holy Scripture.

We are equipped for such a stance through Christ's grace from God's own armoury. In divine power we oppose Schwenckfeld together with his false *Judgement.* This power is the sword of the Spirit as God's Word. In Rev. 19 Christ himself is that Word. Through the might of his Holy Spirit in true believers – his apostles, his true church – he has reformed and built up Christendom and restored it as the sacrament of the New Testament.[144] Even today, he upholds this reformation and edification through his believers, who are his members, his congregation, until he comes in judgement. We are witnesses of the fact that whoever keeps and does the sacraments Christ declared and taught according to his commandment is alone Christ's true disciple, such a one and no one else. According to the Lord's word, "If you remain in my teaching, you are my true disciples and will know the truth" (John 8). This applies only to those who hold to this God. As John writes, "Whoever trespasses and does not remain in Christ's teaching has no God" (2 John 1).

Such speeches of Christ belong indivisibly to our salvation and true devotion. You can't distinguish between them. It doesn't say, "If you remain in my discourse about internals," or, "Whoever trespasses and doesn't remain with Christ's teaching concerning internals." Rather, it states discourses and teaching, to be understood as internal and external without cutting it in half. We long to remain in this school of Christ's teaching. . . . [L. 569/9-48]

. . . Christ commands his apostles to teach and baptize all peoples, teaching them to observe all things he has commanded them (Matt. 28). He gives a whole commandment and not half a one. Schwenckfeld brings up another teaching, saying, "One should devoutly strive after the general commandments of Christ." We know of no general or particular commandment of Christ which believers are not to follow. There is no other reformation, no other way of reforming the church and the sacraments of the New Testament than the way in which Christ himself has set it right and effects it in all true believers. We do not wish to pursue other paths; by his grace we want to remain in the fear and love of the Lord, in his blessed will, in his whole and undivided teaching until the end, that we might be saved (Matt. 24). We pray to the Lord to aid us to that end.

We find it nowhere written that Christ has made the sacraments he instituted invalid, or abolished them so that they now need to be brought into force again. He did not make them valid again so no one else has a need to do so. We should stand firm until his return regardless of who undertakes to invalidate, abolish, abandon, or prohibit them.

Schwenckfeld's advice is shocking to hear! *"If only we had let the water of baptism remain a free sign of repentance and put a moratorium on the Lord Christ's baptism. Instead, we should look more to the new birth and the renewal of the heart, truly teaching this rather than looking to outward things. Then we would have come a long way in God's eyes."*

That tallies perfectly! Show us, Schwenckfeld, where we called our baptism mere "water" or "pouring." But if it is our commandment and not heaven's and doesn't issue from faith in Christ, then it is a human commandment, able to be rejected. How can it then be a "free" sign? And if, as is the case, the water of baptism is from heaven, issuing from the Lord's instruction and our faith, how could we let it be a free sign or make a sign of repentance out of it? How could we put a moratorium on the Lord's order to baptize and let ourselves be led astray by Schwenckfeld from the path of obedience to Christ? For our souls' salvation we must stay true to the indivisible commandments and teachings of Christ concerning baptism, the Lord's Supper, and other things.

And where in the Holy Scriptures of the New Testament are we told to make a baptism of repentance out of a Gospel filled with grace? [L. 570/ *13-571/7*] . . . Christ the Lord gave his apostles quite another commandment. They were to preach not only repentance but a Gospel filled with grace, salvation revealed and present today as forgiveness of sins through the death and blood of Christ. They should baptize those who believe their preaching but not as John did for repentance and sorrow for sin. Rather, it should be for the forgiveness and release of repentant sinners,[145] those who were led to sorrow for their sins by the law and the precursor role of John and have received forgiveness of sins. When they were made ready and worthy they were baptized. Besides the preaching of a grace-filled Gospel . . . we admonished people to repentance and conversion because these must precede forgiveness.

Yet their baptism is not into remorse, regret, or sadness but into comfort, forgiveness, peace, and joy of conscience in the Holy Spirit in the name of the Holy Trinity. In faith they take up the consoling good news, for which they waited with yearning: forgiveness of sin through the shed blood of Christ. Instead of baptizing people into remorse and regret, the apostles baptized them into peace, joy, and comfort. We should too. Where people are baptized upon faith in the forgiveness of sins, there can no longer be a baptism of remorse as in the time of John before the death, resurrection, and ascension of Christ and the giving of the promised Holy Spirit. Now the Lord Christ baptizes with the Consoler of consciences and with assurance of salvation.[146] John's preaching attests to the fact that no one had yet been so baptized. His speeches point to Christ who, he says, will baptize with the Holy Spirit (Matt. 3; Mark. 1; Luke 3; John 1). John neither spoke nor baptized with the Holy Spirit as if the Spirit were already present alongside John's baptism. When he said, "He will baptize with the Holy Spirit," it is to be understood to mean after Christ's death, resurrection, and ascension, and the reception of the promised Holy Spirit. The Lord himself testifies that he has not baptized before his death, because it is after his resurrection that he gives the apostles to understand that they would baptize with the Holy Spirit after his ascension. . . . [L. 571/*18-51*]

... The present age is not only a time for the repentance of sins but for their forgiveness through faith, as we have described it. Therefore, apostolic baptism in not the same as John [the Baptist's] baptism of repentance; apostolic baptism is for the forgiveness and washing away of sins (Acts 2). Penitent, sick, and heavy-laden hearts need no longer wait for sanctification. There is no in between time: holiness has been prepared for today (Matt. 11). The Lord gives forgiveness in exchange for our repentance. The Lord, the human being Christ, received his power from God the Father. He gave his apostles the might to forgive (Matt. 16; John 20). To that extent the offices and baptisms of John the Baptist and the apostles are different from each other. ... [L. 572/*43*-573/*3*]

... We would like to have testimony from Holy Scripture to the effect that the baptism Christ commanded has been suspended and the baptism of contrition has been made a sign of repentance again and commanded anew. Should such baptism as "a sign of repentance," as Schwenckfeld calls it, happen in the name of Christ? In his Spirit he sent a comforter, not an afflicter! The baptism he commanded is not one of sorrow and anxiety but of forgiveness, comfort, and a conscience set at peace. Should one make people who have been set free from their sins go back to the law and the wrath of God (Rom. 7)? Wouldn't that mean taking joy, comfort, and freedom and placing them in the prison house of sorrow and sadness? Then forgiven sins would again trouble a restless conscience and open wounds which Christ our only physician, the giver of peace and joy, has healed. ... [L. 573/*39*-574/*2*]

... Almost the only concern Schwenckfeld had in writing his opinionated *Judgement* was to push his views, even though they are contrary to all foundations of truth. Our description of the baptism Christ instituted and the apostles put into practice to gather and unite all true Christian churches stands in his way. Therefore, the enemy of truth longs to put a moratorium in place in the form of a baptism of repentance and to suspend Christ's other commissions and bring them into doubt. He keeps them waiting on another alleged Johannine baptism and time of repentance, and pointing them to another commissioning, so that the consolation of conscience and true salvation is abolished. Therefore, he is set on dividing the single Christian baptism in two: he has fashioned a specific water baptism without the Holy Spirit. But without faith in Christ, indeed, without an inner working of the Spirit, there is no baptism of the sort we have often attested to.

In sum, it may be seen that through prophets to the Gentiles – like the ones who came to the Jews – the time of the Gentiles is fulfilled (Luke 21). These incidents testify to the fulfillment – or at least its approach. The Jews, as a vexation to the cross of Christ, wait for the sending of another messiah, and have been deceived until today. Just so, a single Christian baptism has become a vexation to the Gentiles. They have become agitated and quarrelsome. Now only a remnant will be saved, that is, a few Gentiles and a few Jews. These thickheaded prophets hold people back from believing the truth, and tell them to wait, to their own ruin – like the Jews – on another commissioning. We readily believe Schwenckfeld because he has a tottering, uncertain conscience, as he himself testifies. He leads others' consciences to doubt salvation in Christ. He accuses us of not having freedom and certainty of conscience but he has neither in his understanding of baptism and communion, either in celebrating it or knowing the true feast of the Lord's Supper. If he is not certain of the forgiveness of sins through Christ's blood with comfort, peace, and joy in the Holy Spirit, how much less is he able to believe. He's caught in the illusion that repentance by itself leads to faith. . . . For that reason, it's no wonder that he opposes a single, true, and undivided baptism in his false *Judgement.*

Neither is he right when he says that we should leave the Lord Christ's baptismal commandment in peace and put a moratorium on it. He states that we should put more weight on the new birth and the renewing of the heart than on outward events. If we had faithfully taught and fostered these, we would be much farther along in God's eyes. Rather, he should have said, if we had diminished or suspended baptism we would be farther from God, the new birth, and the renewing of the heart. That would be hard to believe, since he trespasses against Christ's teaching! The inner and the outer are simply not divided or distinguished in Scripture. . . . [L. 574/*20-575/18*]

. . . We look as much to the inner reality – the new birth and the renewing of the heart in the power of faith in Christ – as to the outer. We have faithfully taught and fostered God's inner working, as we have abundantly shown. Our spirit witnesses with God's Spirit, as does our earlier booklet, that the outward is nothing without the inward. But the outer matters, like baptism and the Lord's Supper, belong to the inner; together they have been ordained by Christ for believers and instituted for faith. Schwenckfeld wants to turn us away from Christ. . . . He states that we should not entangle our conscience but let the matter rest in the Lord and his Holy Spirit. We should look to the inner. By grace we agree that the inner must have pre-eminence. But that does not mean that we should neglect Christ's teaching on outward things and have no conscience on the matter, as Schwenckfeld holds. The inner must be kept undivided from the outer – that was the purpose of Christ's institution. Anything which does not further this is deception. There is no truth in the claim that we value the outer either more or less than the inner. We teach only that the outer serves the inner, otherwise it would follow that we fear and defer to the lowly servant. This would be contrary to the Lord himself who commands both the inner effect ("all in all," Col. 3) and the outer for the good of believers. Why would you suspend outward practices or neglect to foster them toward God and on God's behalf if they are used according to Christ's command? . . . [L. *575/24-576/2*]

. . . Then you could no longer have outer preaching and teaching, for that is also an outer institution of Christ (Matt. 28; Mark 16).[147] And so, if the Holy Spirit came into the heart by faith (Gal. 3), he would not be able to propel the mind and heart of the believer to outward practices which belong to believers and have been instituted by Christ. Is it too hard for the Holy Spirit, who moves the children of God to obey all the teachings of Christ, whether they be inner or outer (Rom. 8)? . . . [L. *576/7-15*]

. . . One of the reasons for Schwenckfeld's false *Judgement*, which we mentioned in the preface, is the scandal and offence of the cross which has fallen upon Christ and his own. They have held to the institutions of Christ, foremost of which is true Christian baptism. This is what Schwenckfeld seeks refuge from. He puts baptism into another form, that of a baptism of repentance, like the circumcision the Jews in Paul's time tried to force on the Galatians. They did so only to avoid persecution for the cross of Christ (Gal. 6). Because the cross offended and scandalized them they turned rather to human praise and forsook the praise of God. . . . The leading Jews acted this way (John 12), though we should seek only the praise which comes from God (John 5). That is like Schwenckfeld, who sets out to distort and disperse, to internalize everything so that God is inwardly pleased and people are outwardly pleased. He wanted to be spared the true offence of Christ's cross and remain in people's good graces. He sees how they abuse, dishonour, mock, and crucify those whom they call "Anabaptists" while he and his adherents are not greatly reviled or hated.[148] . . . [L. *576/31-577/2*]

. . . Where is it written that Christ and his apostles taught a moratorium on Christ's institutions because of untimely persecution? There is never a good time for the flesh because persecution is contrary to it. If you had a moratorium, you'd always be waiting for the "right" time to obey. Paul says we are bound to obey: preach the evangelical word concerning the inner and the outer. Persist in season and out (2 Tim. 4)! Several years ago we asked why some people do not reach for and pursue the things commanded by Christ. They turn to reason. "Well, you must go forward properly and conveniently; wait a while." They are still going forward bit by bit but they never catch up with Christ. They become fixed in position, mostly because they remain exempt from Christ's persecution, cross, and offence. In the meanwhile, many people concerned with the truth become neglectful of Christ's commandments, press for a moratorium, and thereby bring about their own ruin. They will miss out on the future glory because of their own fleshly mindset. Those who suffer with Christ, bearing his offence and affliction, are promised this glory (Rom. 8; Luke 6; 2 Tim. 2). Against God's word and in disobedience to Christ's teaching, they make a moratorium. In so doing, they trespass against God's prohibition. We are to turn neither to the left nor to the right from following the word of God.

From the time of his conversion, calling, and baptism Paul began to exercise his apostolic office, and immediately persecution befell him. His disciples had to let him down over a wall in a basket (Acts 9)! It was the same with the other apostles: when they received the promised Holy Spirit, they began to preach and baptize right away. The reviling and mocking that had been done to Christ speedily became their lot (Acts 2). Twice they were imprisoned because of the cross of Christ. Yet the very hour they were released, they started preaching again! Concerning their imprisonment, punishment, and prohibition against preaching (Acts 4, 5), Schwenckfeld asserts that they brought this untimely persecution upon themselves. . . . [L. 571/27-578/11]

. . . By the grace of God we leave all these matters to the discretion of those who truly believe, who fear God, and who are taught by the Spirit in Christ. Amen. [L. 578/43-45]

# Notes

[1] Marpeck is concerned here with symbol and sign when they are used to separate the sign and the reality signified. The whole burden of his argument from *A Clear Refutation* (his tract of 1531, Klassen & Klaassen, 43-67) onward is that in the incarnation sign and reality are inseparable. This is prolonged in the church and all its outward manifestations. Both in the *Admonition* and the *Response* he uses Augustine's definition of a sacrament as "a visible sign of an invisible grace" on the assumption that the two are part of one reality. For full publication details of the Neff and Klassen and Klassen texts cited in this chapter, see page 18, note 1 of this present volume.

[2] Here Marpeck starts to develop his notion of "sign" and "thing signified" (or the reality itself). This nomenclature originated with Augustine and remained part of ordinary theological discourse into the sixteenth century. In this case, the sign is particular acts of love; the thing signified by them is the incarnation – love and grace in the flesh.

[3] Both Marpeck and Schwenckfeld refer to their own and each other's writing in the folio form in which they then appeared. All those which are printed in modern editions will be listed from those editions. The quotation here is from the *Admonition* Neff, 204, Klassen & Klaassen, 190.

[4] Neff, 208, Klassen & Klaassen, 196. Marpeck makes reference to subdivisions in the original folio, such as D.IV, but these divisions are not carried over in the modern German or English printings.

[5] The purity of a Christian consists in the harmonious union of spirit and flesh.

[6] Here again Marpeck's point seems to be that the water of baptism is *not* a sign (that is, something separate from the essence) but part of the single reality through which God acts.

[7] Neff, 191, Klasssen & Klassen, 169, Answer. Marpeck seldom uses the word "sacrament" but when he does so it is in the Augustinian sense mentioned above.

[8] Here as elsewhere, Marpeck establishes a dynamic in which several elements are necessary for grace to fulfill its intention: water joined to the word which is preached and believed. Some theologians from highly sacramental traditions claim that God's initiative and objective presence are undermined if their working is made conditional on the presence of faith. For Marpeck the sacrament is precisely that point where grace visibly manifested is received by faith. The implication of this claim goes in two directions. First, it challenges the medieval Catholic teaching on sacraments, *ex opere operato*, that the sign achieves what it signifies independent of its reception by faith. This, according to Marpeck, is not a true sacrament. Second, it confronts the spiritualist view (and one which verges on being the *de facto* definition of a sacrament in some Free Church circles) that the outward action is a merely a human one. According to Marpeck, this too is a false understanding of baptism and the Lord's Supper, and likewise not a sacrament. The same criticism is applied to both views: each one is half a sacrament – either a divine or human action but not the point of intersection between both.

[9] John 13.

[10] In response #10.

[11] 1 Cor. 3, 4.

[12] In the prayer Marpeck makes parenthetical reference to responses # 9, 10, and 1 Cor. 3, 4.

[13] In this slight turn of phrase we see one important part of Marpeck's position. He is convinced that Schwenckfeld is concerned only with words and neglects outward actions, and that he confesses God only in the privacy of his own devotion rather in public.

[14] The word "gift" has been inserted because it is implied. This sentence sounds like a liturgical response uttered in the service by the candidate after the baptismal question, perhaps from Acts 8, and before the act of baptism.

[15] The reference is to Neff, 206, Klassen & Klaassen, 193, but Schwenckfeld does not quote Marpeck verbatim. I am puzzled by the translation in Klassen & Klaassen of *frumm* as "good." Conventionally, it means "pious." With Marpeck's emphasis on obedience it might well be translated as "holiness [of life]," and I have done so.

[16] *Ibid.*

[17] Is Marpeck speaking sarcastically here? His re-assertion of this argument in the next paragraph makes this interpretation possible. On the other hand, he seems (here and elsewhere) to wince when Schwenckfeld charges him with an attachment to the outer world which decays and perishes. Later on, Marpeck makes it clear that his attachment is to a spiritual body and not a fleshly one, both as concerns the nature of the church and the presence of Christ in the Lord's Supper.

[18] This dense train of thought becomes a significant summary statement of Marpeck's ecclesiology and soteriology. Each member and the whole body of Christ literally incarnates him in time and space. The created order of things, including our day-to-day existence in the world, can become extensions of God's presence here and now. When we are indwelled by the Spirit, we co-operate with God in bringing the world salvation. This is a parallel thought to that of co-witness, in which persons of the Trinity as well as people and things are drawn into a dynamic which makes salvation present. The leaders of the church are not merely self-appointed managers of a fleshly institution but extensions of the body of Christ and the work of the Spirit. For Schwenckfeld the outer world is decaying and incapable of bearing grace; for Marpeck the outer world as it is manifested in the church is redeemed and participates in the bringing of salvation.

[19] This reference goes back to an earlier exchange between Schwenckfeld and Marpeck. Loserth quotes the former's reference (Epistolar, I, 801-16, reprinted in CS IV, 237-253) to the otherwise unknown treatise of Marpeck, "Vom neuen Menschen" (Concerning the New Person), 126.

[20] Patripassianism is the heresy which claims that God as God suffers in Jesus' suffering.

[21] Neff, 211, Klassen & Klaassen, 200.

[22] The word "knowledge" is not in the text but is implied.

[23] Neff, 208, Klassen & Klaassen, 195.

[24] In this verse, Jesus heals a paralytic. This act is prototypical of the outward action of the Son: he is God present in history. Yet inwardly the Father is active in the paralytic through the Spirit.

[25] This is Marpeck's argument with Schwenckfeld in a nutshell!

[26] Marpeck does not confine himself to conventional lists of sacraments, either Catholic or Protestant. He includes any action which manifests Christ in and through the church. This undertaking is not without precedent in the sixteenth century (Luther) or in the medieval church before the twelfth century. It was only then that a long list of sacramental actions was reduced to seven in the Western church.

[27] Neff, 191-92, Klassen & Klaassen, 169-71.

[28] The preceding sentences provide one of the few direct references in the *Response* to liturgical practice. What Marpeck describes here is often called "receptionism," the claim that the power of a sacrament lies in the faith of the recipient. Marpeck counts not only the faith of the candidate but also of the congregation and minister. At the same time, the event of grace happens through God's initiative, "the Father inwardly through the Spirit and the Son outwardly." These three claims – especially the first and third – stand side by side in Marpeck's thinking but they are never assimilated into a single, embracing concept.

[29] Neff, 207, Klassen & Klaassen, 194.

[30] Here Marpeck accuses Schwenckfeld of realized eschatology, i.e., that believers are no longer subject to the constraints of creatureliness. For Schwenckfeld, sacramental life became superfluous with Christ and the new birth. For Marpeck, sacramental life makes Christ and the new birth at home in history.

[31] The German term is *Erbsuende*, inherited sin, generally taken to be the equivalent of "original sin" in English. There is a difference, however. The German emphasizes how we enter the sinful state, that is, by inheritance.

[32] This is what Marpeck writes, *verbatim*. He seems to be referring to two of Augustine's related teachings. The first is that even within marriage making love is sinful. The second is that Adam's sin is passed from generation to generation through sexual intercourse.

[33] Here Marpeck is consistent with his presuppositions. He refuses to take refuge in either of two theological claims which arose to safeguard Christ from participating in fallen humanity. One is the immaculate conception of Mary, the other is the doctrine of Christ's celestial flesh, which Schwenckfeld, Hoffmann, and Menno took over from popular Catholic theology of the time.

[34] Neff. 214-18; 241, Klassen & Klaassen, 205-10; 244-45.

[35] The German word *vernunft* can be translated equally as understanding, reason, discernment, or common sense. "Understanding" is the common theological translation of the word but it might well have a rational tinge to it not intended by Marpeck.

[36] The connotation of simplicity is innocence. Marpeck uses the same word to translate "wise as serpents and innocent as doves" in this section of the text (Matt. 10).

[37] Marpeck says only *sich selbs* (themselves), but a contrast between true and false human nature is implied.

[38] Klassen & Klaassen, 208. This is the obvious reference but Marpeck does not

quote himself *verbatim*: "... believe, confess, and desire baptism." The German leaves out the word "baptism" but it is implied (Neff, 217).

[39] The modern German translation of *gegenerb* is *Miterbe* or "co-heir." A case could be made for the literal translation of *gegenerb* as "counter-inheritance" – grace as the counterpoint to sin.

[40] These words do not appear in Deut. 33, but it is a chapter full of blessings by Moses.

[41] The reference is in error. There is no chapter 37 in Numbers (or in Deuteronomy) in either the German or English Bible.

[42] Marpeck seems to be saying here that a "natural" relationship with God is possible, i.e., that in a spiritually receptive person there need not be an existential "fall" in which all capacity to respond to God is lost. There is an inescapable allusion here to the train of thought, if not the actual text, of Rom. 2:6-16.

[43] Marpeck says *unwirklich*, which means "inoperable." Taken literally it contradicts the sense of the sentence. I take it to mean "untouched" by the power of darkness.

[44] In German, *gespons* can mean either bride or bridegroom, so I have used the term "spouse."

[45] There is the suggestion here that the humanity of the believer is like that of the ascended Christ: a physical body but in a spiritual manner.

[46] This paragraph is of utmost significance for Marpeck's argument because here he tries to synthesize several usages of "flesh" and its equivalent "body." First, he makes John 6 a eucharistic text, with the same reference point as the institutional narratives in the Synoptics and Paul. Thus, John 6 is a sacramental text and not only a mystical one. Over the centuries this claim remained contested. Marpeck's reading of this crucial text lines up all the potentially eucharistic texts in the NT on the sacramental side of the argument. He goes on to tie these texts to those concerning the incarnation and the church as the body of Christ. Christ became flesh of our flesh so that we might become flesh of his flesh. Even though in the new birth (as was the case before the fall) our bodies are given a supernatural form, they remain part of the created order of things. The implication of this line of thought is that in the Lord's Supper there is a communion of the physical body of Christ in "supernatural form."

[47] Neff, 217, Klassen & Klaassen, 209-10.

[48] The convolutions of thought expressed in these paragraphs remind the reader that for people like Marpeck, who was already under suspicion of sedition, it was an excruciating undertaking to speak honestly but fairly about worldly rulers. Being a Christian and exercising armed power is probably a harder thought for Marpeck to conceive of than it is for Schwenckfeld. For the former, Christ's reign on earth is historical, or embodied, much like that of a worldly government. For the latter, Christ's reign is a-temporal and spiritual: the demands of each master are so different that they do not conflict with each other.

[49] Neff, 228: Schwenckfeld makes further reference in the margin to 229-31; Klassen & Klaassen, 225-26.

[50] Neff, 264, Klassen & Klaassen, 276-77.

[51] Marpeck writes *Philippo dem Sibner*, that is, "Philip. one of the seven."

[52] Neff, 255-56, Klassen & Klaassen, 264-65.

[53] Neff, 244; 255-56, Klassen & Klaassen, 249; 264 (not verbatim); 265. The quotations are all from the *Admonition*. From Marpeck's own footnotes it is clear that this treatise was published not as a single text but in folios with separate identification letters and numbers.

[54] Marpeck has misread Schwenckfeld in Paragraph 91 (Loserth, 432). The latter claimed the words in question as his own correct statement about a true Supper. Now Marpeck claims and interprets them as his own.

[55] Schwenckfeld uses the term *wirt*, meaning host, family head, or innkeeper. It is unclear whether the reference here or below is to Christ or to the presiding minister or the householder at whose home the service is held. The former is more likely, because later on in the same passage Marpeck asserts that love comes from knowing the host.

[56] Neff, 261-62, Klassen & Klaassen, 272-75.

[57] Neff, 261-62, Klassen & Klaassen, 272-75.

[58] Here is the most succinct statement of one of Marpeck's foundational claims: God is immediately present and revealed not only in the faith but in the works of believers. This assertion is the frame of reference for Marpeck's often repeated claim that it is the faith of the church and the believer which makes bread and wine into a sacramental reality. Since faith comes wholly from the Spirit, one could say that the Spirit, by means of our faith, is the agent of Christ's presence in the Supper.

[59] The argument there and later concerns idolatry as presented in 1 Cor. 10:14ff.

[60] Neff, 259, 270, Klassen & Klaassen, 269 and 285, according to Loserth's footnote, but both statements above are not *verbatim* quotations but elaborate on the fragments quoted from the *Admonition*.

[61] Neff, 192, Klassen & Klaassen, 171. Here and elsewhere Marpeck quotes himself but abbreviates what he said in the original text.

[62] Neff, 272-74, Klassen & Klaassen, 288-91.

[63] Neff, 272-74, Klassen & Klaassen, 288-91.

[64] The above words, and others like them, have the character of a formula and might have been words of invitation at the celebration of the Lord's Supper. They have a remarkable similarity to a part of the "Pledge of Love" in Balthasar Hubmaier's communion service in *Balthasar Hubmaier: Theologian of Anabaptism*, H. Pipkin, J.H. Yoder, ed. and trans. (Scottdale: Herald Press, 1989), 403-04.

[65] Marpeck regularly repeats this emphasis. Historically, it is known as "receptionism," meaning that the effect (not the cause) of the sacrament is in its believing reception. Martin Bucer, Marpeck's Reformed debating partner in Strasbourg, and Thomas Cranmer, the architect of the Anglican *Book of Common Prayer*, held similar views. It is noteworthy that Marpeck places this emphasis side by side with some of his strongest claims for the real presence of Christ in the Supper, e.g., above, "eating and

drinking of the flesh and blood of Jesus Christ." Not the breaking of bread in and of itself but its reception in a community gathered in faith and love is a communion with Christ.

[66] Neff, 270, Klassen &Klaassen, 286. In our text Marpeck seems to be saying that he is quoting Franck, but in the *Admonition* this fact is not noted. It is probably a direct quotation because its interpretation is sacramentally weaker than Marpeck usually holds to; that is, it is the believer who acts rather than the Holy Spirit as a co-witness with the believer.

[67] This statement is surprising, because Franck permits a parallelism between partaking the bread and receiving the body which Marpeck's earlier formulations are carefully crafted to avoid. Marpeck is emphatic about the inseparability of the inner and outer events, at the same time being careful not to conflate them as popular understandings of transubstantiation did. Is Marpeck trying to use Franck, an erstwhile ally of Schwenckfeld, to make his own position less odious to Schwenckfeld?

[68] Folio N (Loserth notes that it is actually the conclusion of Folio M) Neff, 272, Klassen & Klaassen, 289.

[69] Marpeck seems to be struggling here, as he often is, to appease people who attack any sacramental claim as an assertion of a corporeal presence. At the same time, he is saying more and more elaborately, as the nature of debate concerning the Eucharist is clarified, that through the action of the Spirit and the faith of communicants, the elements become part of a communion of the body and blood of Christ.

[70] These two notions re-echo in some contemporary theologies of the Lord's Supper where the emphasis is on the 'finished work of Christ' not only as his death but also his exaltation and continued intercession for the world. The emphasis on the Holy Spirit's immediate action in the breaking of bread is central to Orthodox eucharistic claims as well as the theology behind *Baptism, Eucharist, and Ministry, Faith and Order #111* (Geneva: World Council of Churches, 1982).

[71] This quotation conflates words from 1 Cor. with Matt. 26:26.

[72] According to the *Testamentserleüterung*, ch. 87, under the title "bread today," folios 272, 273.

[73] This seems to be a reference to Rom. 8:15.

[74] Loserth notes this seeming contradiction, 467.

[75] Marpeck echoes in agreement with the soaring words of John 6. Then he backs off to emphasize the "mere" sign character of the Supper yet concluding that the food Christ offers sustains not only the soul but also the body unto eternal life. Marpeck often writes as if his harshest critic is looking over his shoulder. It is difficult to tell whether he is easily swayed or whether he realizes that the stakes are so high that every eventuality must be planned for. The consequence of Marpeck's willingness to appease is that his thought never reaches a self-confident synthesis. Each argument remains bound to the immediate circumstance which occasioned it.

[76] According to Loserth, the reference is to Neff, 262, Klassen & Klaassen, 275, but it is not an exact quotation.

[77] "Vom erkantnus Christi" is a collection of articles, according to Loserth (471). The above quotation is taken from the article, "Ermanunge zum waren und

seligmachenden erkanthnus Christi" (Admonition to a true and saving knowledge of Christ), written in 1539. In making his case against Marpeck, Schwenckfeld uses the term "carnal" (*fleischlich*) as the equivalent of Marpeck's "bodily" (*leiblich*). The former implies that matter remains in the realm of sin; the latter implies that for believers it is part of the realm of spirit. The debaters are unable to acknowledge their different starting points.

[78] This is the point on which Marpeck's christology, ecclesiology, and sacramentology turns. The incarnation, God's participation in the world through his embrace of our flesh, remains his primal expression of revelation, love, and grace. The medium of his saving presence is the "flesh," the historical person of Jesus, prolonged in his body the church, manifested in the sacraments.

[79] Marpeck's christological formulations place great emphasis on relationships within the Trinity and describe the co-ordination in which they work. He talks about the oneness of Christ's two natures and how his humanness has become part of the Godhead. At other times, as here, he seems to conflate the work and nature of Christ in his divine nature with the Holy Spirit. Two recent works which grapple with intratrinitarian relationships deal with aspects of Marpeck's agenda. See J. Zizioulas, *Being as Communion* (London: Darton, Longman, & Todd, 1985), esp. 110ff, 123ff, 210ff, and J. Moltmann, *History and the Triune God* (New York: Crossroads, 1992), esp. 66ff and 86ff.

[80] This is one of the trickiest aspects of Marpeck's argument. His goal is to claim the presence and power of Christ's saving death in and for history. This presence is ritually claimed in the Supper. It is hard to tell which is the chicken and which the egg at this juncture. Does Marpeck emphasize that Christ's human body is corporeally located in heaven until he comes again so that it cannot be corporeally located in the bread, against Catholics and Lutherans? Or does he insist on the spiritual presence of Christ's body to overcome the argument of some radical reformers who insist that Christ's human body is in every way localized in heaven? Or, has he created this argument only to counter the Spiritualists, like Schwenckfeld, to claim that bread and wine effectively signify the real presence of Christ within time and space, but are spiritually received?

[81] Marpeck has built up his eucharistic argument almost entirely from the fourth Gospel. He uses John 6 as words of institution, as on par with, if not loftier than, those in the Synoptics and Paul.

[82] Marpeck's argument is repetitive and forceful almost to the point of obsession. He believed that nothing less than the incarnation was under threat from Schwenckfeld's spiritualism and that without the incarnation there could be no atonement. The flavour of his writing is not unlike that of Justin and Irenaeus, in the early patristic era, when they defended the incarnation and the Lord's Supper against the Gnostics.

[83] This paragraph, the essence of which is that in the Supper we receive the incarnate body of Christ, spiritually given to us, is Marpeck's most succinct description of the nature of the "real presence."

[84] Both men want nothing more than to make clear to people that reconciliation with God comes through Christ's saving death. But they are talking past each other. Listen to Marpeck's quotation of Schwenckfeld two paragraphs further along. "I could find no consolation . . . in God if my disobedience had not been atoned for by his Son's obedience

on the cross . . ., if I had not been born again through his Holy Spirit." The debate is relentless because each believes the other has falsified the message. Each has touched a nerve on the other, i.e., challenged a concept on which the structure of each respective theology is grounded.

[85] In our text Marpeck often uses the virgin birth to reinforce the complete humanity of Christ. One senses that as a medieval Christian he finds it hard to use Mary as an argument for Jesus' full humanity, i.e., that he was born to a woman who was a sinner like all other mortals. In this passage he is less equivocal about that claim than he is in other places.

[86] A paraphrase of John 6:50-58.

[87] Both men have the same passion, to proclaim the saving sacrifice of Christ and let its indwelling power transform human lives. Marpeck quotes a moving passage from Schwenckfeld which makes this clear. "I would have no consolation in God or his grace if his Son's obedience on the cross . . . had not atoned for my disobedience. . . . If his death had not gained for me rebirth through the Holy Spirit I would have remained eternally damned and lost." (*Cathechismus vom Worte des Kreuzes*, CS IX, 448-93, esp. 455). The two men talk past each other in their attempts to describe how the Lord's Supper manifests the life of grace. Marpeck's preoccupation is to show forth the incarnation of Christ as the means of redeeming the flesh. Schwenckfeld's concern is to show forth the triumph of Christ over the flesh. The goal of Marpeck's convoluted christology is to transcend what he perceived to be two erroneous extremes: (1) Luther's view in which Christ is present in the breaking of bread in both natures and is eaten corporeally; (2) Schwenckfeld's position in which Christ is also present in both natures but without visible evidence because he has left his incarnate self behind.

[88] Marpeck is here paving the way for a distinction he will unfold later in the *Response*. There he says that the church is the prolongation of Christ's untransfigured body of flesh and blood. At the end of time it will similarly become the prolongation of his transfigured body. For Marpeck the church on earth is physical, outward, historical; for Schwenckfeld the church already exists on a purely spiritual plane.

[89] Earlier Marpeck's focus was the present *earthly* ministry of Christ in continuity with the incarnation. There he formulated a parallelism, "the Father works inwardly though the Spirit as the Son works outwardly." Now his concern is with the *heavenly* ministry of the divine Christ; his agent is the Spirit. The contrast now is between the two works of Christ, in heaven through the Spirit and on earth through the church.

[90] Marpeck is trying to dance at two weddings, i.e., he wants to use the notion "the humanity of Christ" in two ways, first (one of his great acts of theological imagination) the church, second the human body of the individual, Christ. He needs to locate the latter firmly in heaven so he cannot be accused of claiming Christ's corporeal, local presence in the Eucharist.

[91] Marpeck seems to be referring to John 1:18. The intended reference in Timothy is obscure.

[92] It is unclear whether the reference is to Christ as the second person of the Trinity or to his body the church. The logic of the passage suggests the latter.

[93] This is not a verbatim quotation but the idea can be found in CS, III, 387.

⁹⁴ Marpeck often speaks in doublets. He joins two words with "or," letting the meaning of one add to that of the other. In this case "person" and "body" are not joined by "or" but by "and," suggesting that he is referring here to the human individual, Jesus, and to his body the church.

⁹⁵ Marpeck's concern for the heavenly ministry of the divine Christ helps toward a broad concept of salvation. It consists not only of Jesus' earthly healing ministry nor only of his atoning death. As the ascended Lord, Jesus continues the saving work he began on earth. He intercedes for us (Hebrews) and continually sends the Holy Spirit (John).

⁹⁶ The reference here is probably to the Apostles' Creed.

⁹⁷ Col. 1:19 is the unmistakable reference here. This part of the argument has few direct Biblical allusions.

⁹⁸ Because of the denseness of the concepts being laid out in these sections and because proper nouns are not often, but occasionally, capitalized in sixteenth-century German, it is not easy to determine Marpeck's reference for "word." He almost never capitalizes it, but in this text he makes it clear that he is referring to the Word of God as the second person of the Trinity in the Johannine sense.

⁹⁹ Even though Marpeck avoids binitarianism with this formulation – Word and Spirit share the same power, but as distinct persons – he ends up with a christological split: Christ in his divinity works inwardly "into the inner ear"; Christ in his humanity works outwardly, through the actions of the church. For Marpeck's reference to Schwenckfeld's Catechism, Loserth (513) refers to Folio A III, Orthodoxe Bücher, 568 A, *Das Wort des Kreuz* (The Word of the Cross) and *vom* (sic) *Unterschaid des Worts des Geists und Buechstabens* (On the Distinction between the Word of the Spirit and the Letter).

¹⁰⁰ As usual, Marpeck is working within a Johannine frame of reference (especially chapters 14 to 16) but in this section he makes two departures. First, it is now the Son who sends the Spirit. Marpeck makes this claim in order to emphasize the prerogatives of the glorified Christ, even though John says that the sending of the Spirit is the work of the Father with the Son. Secondly, the Spirit comes with the Word. Marpeck's goal in this case seems to be the ongoing work of Christ in his divinity in the world. The "word" which the church speaks and lives today is "the Word," i.e., the bodily word of preaching on earth is one with the transfigured Word in heaven. With this move, Marpeck steps outside the Johannine trinitarian scheme.

¹⁰¹ 1 Thess. 4:13-18.

¹⁰² The Catechism is called *Vom Wort des Kreuz* (Concerning the Word of the Cross). Further reference is made to *Unterschaid des Worts des Geistes und Buchstabens* (The Difference between the Word of Spirit and Letter), CS, IX, 448-93.

¹⁰³ *"Verwerfung des broetinen aus der h. schrifft"* ("The Repudiation of Bread from Holy Scripture") BB II, in manuscript form only, with further details in Loserth, 517.

¹⁰⁴ In the phrase "visible, spiritual sense" Marpeck holds together what Schwenckfeld separates. Their debate in christology and sacramentology turns on this phrase.

¹⁰⁵ Marpeck uses a number of terms to express the oneness of the Trinity. Even the unusual title "God Christ" is intended to say that all of God, Father, Son, and Spirit are

active in revelation. In other places, Marpeck speaks of the work of Christ before his incarnation in creation and in the formation of the Hebrew people.

[106] The debate concerning the written Word of God parallels but is much briefer than the opponents' position on ceremonies. Marpeck disclaims the Word as mere pen and paper but he does contend – without using the word – that the Bible "incarnates" the Word and that its preaching is revelatory. For Schwenckfeld, material reality cannot be revelatory; at best the Bible is an outward record of the Word but unmistakably secondary to its inward illumination.

[107] The following line is inserted at this place in the text but breaks the flow of thought: in John 8:12 and Heb. 1 he calls them the word of God.

[108] Marpeck seems to be saying that God's word is spirit and life in someone only when it is received by faith. Without faith no life is received through externals. But this does not mean that the living word is not present and active; faith is not its cause but the condition of its effectiveness.

[109] Catechism, CS, IX, 464.

[110] Marpeck says the quotation is taken from the Catechism C III but Loserth (530) notes that it is not found there in the CS.

[111] *Vom Erkantnus Christi* (Concerning the Knowledge of Christ), n.p. However, this quotation is Schwenckfeld's own concise summary of longer quotations presented by Marpeck from *Vom klainen bericht* (Concerning a Short Report), CS, III, 390 and *Von der leiblichen stell* (Concerning the Bodily Place), CS, VI, 80-85.

[112] The text says, ". . . that his flesh was creaturely before his death . . ." In German the difference lies in one letter: *kein* rather than *ein*. Unless the statement is taken as it is in my text, it is very difficult to reconcile with Schwenckfeld's other claims and with Marpeck's argument.

[113] The quotation is actually from Heb. 4:14.

[114] Folio C.4, *Confession von Jesu Christi* (Confession of Jesus Christ), Orthodxe Bücher, 294.

[115] This formulation seems to fly in the face of the notion, "what Christ was by nature we become by grace." This statement concerns our divinization. Marpeck's concern is to make a distinction between the first Adam, a natural being, and the second Adam, a spiritual being.

[116] Marpeck is struggling for all he is worth to hold together the true humanity and real body of Christ with his divine origin and sinlessness. The notion of pre-created flesh is very like that of the late medieval "celestial flesh" christology which Schwenckfeld passed on to Melchior Hoffman (and through Hoffman to Menno Simons). While it buttresses the orthodoxy of Marpeck's christology in a narrow sense, it undermines his vigorous teaching on the incarnation and its full participation in the natural order.

[117] Loserth (542) cites Folio HH without further explanation.

[118] There is no obvious reference to Marpeck's theme in this chapter.

[119] The reference is to Acts 2:27.

[120] Marpeck is addressing an age-old question of christology. If Jesus was sinless, could he have fully shared our humanity in his incarnation? Marpeck does not opt for the immaculate conception of Mary, to give Jesus truly human but sinless flesh. He avoids part of the celestial flesh christology (favoured, in variations, by Hoffman, Menno, and Schwenckfeld alike) in which Jesus' unfallen flesh is merely incubated in Mary. Marpeck still insists that Christ's flesh was different from ours but that, by an act of will rather by nature, he embraced our mortality by choosing to die.

[121] The reference is to Rev. 4:5.

[122] This rendering of the text by Marpeck is a very loose paraphrase of Job 19:25.

[123] *Von der anbetung* (Concerning Adoration), CS, VIII, 319-99, esp. 370-71. Loserth notes that the citation is from Ambrose's *De Fide Resur.*, ch. 21 (Loserth, 548).

[124] 1 John 5:7-8 is meant here but what is presented as a quotation goes beyond the Biblical text. In addition, most modern translations claim that the oldest manuscripts say, "spirit, water, and blood."

[125] Here Marpeck requotes Schwenckfeld, *Von der leiblichen stell* (Concerning the Localized Presence), CS, VI, 81.

[126] *Von der mitlung* (Concerning mediation), CS, VIII, 721-23.

[127] The question at issue seems to be this: if the "real Adam" is the fallen person then sin is constitutive of humanness; if the "real Adam" is the unfallen person, then it is not inherited but chosen.

[128] Marpeck's positive view of the original creation and the incarnation lets him affirm our humanness. We need not deprive ourselves of hearth, table, or companionship: they are part of our humanness.

[129] Marpeck has insisted all along that the bodies of believers are spiritual (derived from his preceding claim about the church as the body of Christ). What happens after the resurrection, when believers enter the immediate presence of Christ, completes their humanity by making it like his. See 1 John 3:2 for the possible inspiration for this claim.

[130] The reference here is to 1 Cor. 15:45.

[131] This oneness between the Father and the Son is a *Leitmotiv* of the Johannine writings and is found explicitly in 1 John 2:23.

[132] Neff, 272, Klassen & Klaassen, 287-88.

[133] The quotation is taken from Neff, 272, Klassen & Klaassen, 288, but in the italicized words Marpeck departs from his own text.

[134] The words of institution in the Synoptics and Paul play a minor role in Marpeck's eucharistic – and christological – thought. On both subjects, most of the references throughout have been to the Johannine corpus with side references to Hebrews and Paul's teaching on the resurrection, with the occasional invocation of Isa. 53. What interests Marpeck is the bodily reality of the incarnation, Jesus' suffering as a mortal, and the exaltation of his humanity. The Lord's Supper re-presents the bodily nature of God's redeeming love. It is John who supplies Marpeck with the images of his stock in trade and not the Synoptic account of the Last Supper.

[135] The plot thickens at this point. Marpeck wants to find common ground with Schwenckfeld so he pulls apart exegetical arguments that have heretofore been held loosely together. The institutional narratives have contributed the memorial aspect to his eucharistic theology, while John has made the case for the real presence. Now he contends that the breaking of bread is a figurative action separate from a mystical, unmediated feeding on Christ. Yet the genius of Marpeck's interpretation all along has been the inseparability of these two actions: that is the nature of a sacrament. Marpeck is grappling in the following paragraphs and ends up advancing conflicting arguments.

[136] Neff, 276, Klassen & Klaassen, 294.

[137] This is an extraordinary statement from Marpeck! He is almost making good on his concord with his opponent to speak "without argument or casuistry" (the verb "understand" is still in the conditional). They do, in fact, have much in common in their piety, their love for the fourth Gospel, their yearning for a real communion of the body and blood of Christ. But one cannot escape the sense that Marpeck feels obligated to account for himself to Schwenckfeld. Added to that is the probability that they were appealing to many of the same people seeking a holy life and community in South Germany.

[138] Schwenckfeld has indeed understood Marpeck's earlier claim correctly: At crucial junctures in their debate, Marpeck takes John 6 as a parallel to the institutional narratives in the Synoptics and Paul. At many points Marpeck has insisted that "the essential meal" of Christ is the breaking of bread, the point in time and space where people gather in faith and love and to receive Christ in the sharing of bread and wine. What accounts for the self-contradiction here? In my earlier study of the *Response* (*The Lord's Supper in Anabaptism*) 103 I discounted the theory that the "Marpeck circle" was responsible for this document. But since Marpeck's general position on the Supper and the church is more sacramental than in Anabaptism at large, it could be imagined that a spiritualistically inclined member of his circle – yet pastorally in competition with Schwenckfeld – insisted that John 6 had nothing to do with the sacrament of bread and wine.

[139] This is a grammatically convoluted and novel line of thought. Perhaps it comes from another hand than Marpeck's.

[140] Loserth identifies the quotation as coming from the same location as Klassen & Klaassen, 292; the italicized words are not there but the word in square brackets is there.

[141] Anabaptist leaders.

[142] Marpeck has been stung by Schwenckfeld's accusation that the "baptism brothers" fix their faith on baptism rather than Christ. He is aghast at the fact that Schwenckfeld has re-asserted his plea for a moratorium on ceremonies. The stirrings of a spirit of conciliarity late in their debate have been for naught, from Marpeck's point of view. But Schwenckfeld should not be seen as a scoundrel, because from his point of view they have achieved a breakthrough: they will put a moratorium on outward things and come together on "faith and a virtuous Christian life." Schwenckfeld must have considered the *Admonition* a book to be reckoned with, given the extensiveness of his response. The same can be said of Marpeck. The piety, as much as the theological acumen, of both commanded the other's respect, and made it the more desirable to win such an honourable opponent to one's cause. Marpeck responded to the *Judgement* in the hundred

sections into which he had divided it. It became a living conversation, with detailed attention to the thoughts before him rather than a sweeping response to the whole unfolding of Schwenckfeld's argument. So, when he isolates a point of possible convergence, Marpeck becomes agreeable. Then he explodes with judgmentalism at the next twist in Schwenckfeld's thought, which for Schwenckfeld was genuinely the path to reconciliation.

[143] Here Marpeck pushes Schwenckfeld's position to its logical conclusion. If the essence of the Christian life is inwardness, then not only outward ceremonies but the physical assembling of the body of Christ are optional and easily become a distraction from the individual's relationship with Christ and participation in the mystical, invisible body of Christ.

[144] The lack of consistent noun declensions in sixteenth-century German makes it hard to distinguish singular from plural endings. From the context, it seems clear that the first use of "sacrament" in this paragraph is in the singular. If so, it expresses Marpeck's ecclesiology and sacramentology with poignancy: the church itself is Christ's sacrament.

[145] The word used here is "sin," but "repentant sin" makes no sense, so I have taken it to mean "sinners." Also, in the following clause "they" refers to people and reinforces the reference to people.

[146] On one level the two disputants are talking past each other again. Schwenckfeld is clearly not opposed to a Gospel of grace and assurance, as Marpeck accuses him of being. Yet he does consign outward ceremonies to an old order of things, which has now been superseded. As a concession he has proposed a role for baptism as a sign of human remorse. But it is excluded from any role in the coming of grace. This role for baptism fits nicely into John the Baptist's ministry. But the implication is that with the coming of Christ outward signs become superfluous. This is the claim Marpeck is ultimately trying to refute. For him baptism really only comes of age with the advent of Christ: it brings us consolation and assurance of salvation. In the end, for Marpeck baptism is hard evidence that God keeps his promises: it is a co-witness with faith. God gives us earthly signs because we are earthly creatures. Schwenckfeld, on the other hand, has only his inner receptiveness of soul with which to lay hold of the promises of God. What happens, Marpeck would ask, when that receptiveness of soul is absent?

[147] Marpeck is pressing Schwenckfeld to be consistent. If outward forms have passed away for those who are born again, then surely there is no need for outward teaching. In other words, why should Schwenckfeld have bothered to write the *Judgement*?

[148] Marpeck is someone who cannot bear to listen to certain threatening thoughts. Often, instead of thinking Schwenckfeld's thoughts after him, he simply rails against his opponent. But he has consistently resisted using a weapon of enormous emotional power against Schwenckfeld. It is the fact that the Anabaptists are persecuted because they are visible. They are visible because they believe that the body of Christ is visible and that faith can, and must, be seen in baptism. The spiritualists are much less persecuted because they remain invisible.

# About Pandora Press

Pandora Press is a small, independently owned press dedicated to making available modestly priced books that deal with Anabaptist, Mennonite, and Believers Church topics, both historical and theological. We welcome comments from our readers.

John Driver, *Radical Faith. An Alternative History of the Christian Church*
(Kitchener: Pandora Press, 1999; co-published with Herald Press)
Softcover, 334pp. ISBN 0-9683462-8-6
$32.00 U.S./$35.00 Canadian. Postage: $5.00 U.S./$6.00 Can.
[*A history of the church as it is seldom told – from the margins*]

C. Arnold Snyder, *From Anabaptist Seed.*
*The Historical Core of Anabaptist-Related Identity*
(Kitchener: Pandora Press, 1999; co-published with Herald Press)
Softcover, 53pp.; discussion questions. ISBN 0-9685543-0-X
$5.00 U.S./$6.25 Canadian. Postage: $2.00 U.S./$2.50 Can.
[*Ideal for group study, commissioned by Mennonite World Conference*]

John D. Thiesen, *Mennonite and Nazi? Attitudes Among Mennonite*
*Colonists in Latin America, 1933-1945.*
(Kitchener: Pandora Press, 1999; co-published with Herald Press)
Softcover, 330pp., 2 maps, 24 b/w illustrations, bibliography, index
ISBN 0-9683462-5-1
$25.00 U.S./$28.00 Canadian. Postage: $4.00 U.S./$5.00 Can.
[*Careful and objective study of an explosive topic*]

*Lifting the Veil. Mennonite Life in Russia before the Revolution,*
ed. by Leonard Friesen, trans. by Walter Klaassen
(Kitchener: Pandora Press, 1998; co-published with Herald Press).
Softcover, 128pp., 4pp illustrations ISBN 0-9683462-1-9
$12.50 U.S./$14.00 Canadian. Postage: $4.00 U.S./$4.00 Can.
[*Insightful memoirs of a leading Mennonite pastor and author*]

Leonard Gross, *The Golden Years of the Hutterites, revised edition*
(Kitchener: Pandora Press, 1998; co-published with Herald Press).
Softcover, 280pp., index, one map. ISBN 0-9683462-3-5
$22.00 U.S./$25.00 Canadian. Postage: $4.00 U.S./$5.00 Can.
[*A classic study of the second-generation Hutterites, available again*]

*The Believers Church: A Voluntary Church*, ed. by William H. Brackney (Kitchener: Pandora Press, 1998; co-published with Herald Press). Softcover, viii, 237pp., index. ISBN 0-9683462-0-0 $25.00 U.S./$27.50 Canadian. Postage: $4.00 U.S./$5.00 Can. [*Papers read at the 12th Believers Church Conference, Hamilton, Ont.*]

*An Annotated Hutterite Bibliography*, compiled by Maria H. Krisztinkovich, ed. by Peter C. Erb (Kitchener, Ont.: Pandora Press, 1998). (Ca. 2,700 entries) 312pp., cerlox bound, electronic, or both. ISBN (paper) 0-9698762-8-9/(disk) 0-9698762-9-7 $15.00 each, U.S. and Canadian. Postage: $6.00 U.S. and Can. [*The most extensive bibliography on Hutterite literature available*]

Jacobus ten Doornkaat Koolman, *Dirk Philips. Friend and Colleague of Menno Simons*, trans. W. E. Keeney, ed. C. A. Snyder (Kitchener: Pandora Press, 1998; co-pub. with Herald Press). Softcover, xviii, 236pp., index. ISBN: 0-9698762-3-8 $23.50 U.S./$28.50 Canadian. Postage: $4.00 U.S./$5.00 Can. [*The definitive biography of Dirk Philips, now available in English*]

Sarah Dyck, ed./tr., *The Silence Echoes: Memoirs of Trauma & Tears* (Kitchener: Pandora Press, 1997; co-published with Herald Press). Softcover, xii, 236pp., 2 maps. ISBN: 0-9698762-7-0 $17.50 U.S./$19.50 Canadian. Postage: $4.00 U.S./$5.00 Can. [*First person accounts of life in the Soviet Union, trans. from German*]

Wes Harrison, *Andreas Ehrenpreis and Hutterite Faith and Practice* (Kitchener: Pandora Press, 1997; co-published with Herald Press). Softcover, xxiv, 274pp., 2 maps, index. ISBN 0-9698762-6-2 $26.50 U.S./$32.00 Canadian. Postage: $4.00 U.S./$5.00 Can. [*First biography of this important seventeenth century Hutterite leader*]

C. Arnold Snyder, *Anabaptist History and Theology: Revised Student Edition* (Kitchener: Pandora Press, 1997; co-pub. Herald Press). Softcover, xiv, 466pp., 7 maps, 28 illustrations, index, bibliography. ISBN 0-9698762-5-4 $35.00 U.S./$38.00 Canadian. Postage: $5.00 U.S./$6.00 Can. [*Abridged, rewritten edition for undergraduates and the non-specialist*]

Nancey Murphy, *Reconciling Theology and Science: A Radical Reformation Perspective* (Kitchener, Ont.: Pandora Press, 1997). x, 103pp., index. Softcover. ISBN 0-9698762-4-6
$14.50 U.S./$17.50 Canadian. Postage: $3.50 U.S./$4.00 Can.
[*Exploration of the supposed conflict between Christianity and Science*]

C. Arnold Snyder and Linda A. Huebert Hecht, eds, *Profiles of Anabaptist Women: Sixteenth Century Reforming Pioneers* (Waterloo, Ont.: Wilfrid Laurier University Press, 1996). Softcover, xxii, 442pp. ISBN: 0-88920-277-X
$28.95 U.S. or Canadian. Postage: $5.00 U.S./$6.00 Can.
[*Biographical sketches of more than 50 Anabaptist women; a first*]

*The Limits of Perfection: A Conversation with J. Lawrence Burkholder* 2nd ed., with a new epilogue by J. Lawrence Burkholder, Rodney Sawatsky and Scott Holland, eds. (Kitchener: Pandora Press, 1996). Softcover, x, 154pp. ISBN 0-9698762-2-X
$10.00 U.S./$13.00 Canadian. Postage: $2.00 U.S./$3.00 Can.
[*J.L. Burkholder on his life experiences; eight Mennonites respond*]

C. Arnold Snyder, *Anabaptist History and Theology: An Introduction* (Kitchener: Pandora Press, 1995). Softcover, x, 434pp., 6 maps, 29 illustrations, index, bibliography. ISBN 0-9698762-0-3
$35.00 U.S./$38.00 Canadian. Postage: $5.00 U.S./$6.00 Can.
[*Comprehensive survey; unabridged version, fully documented*]

C. Arnold Snyder, *The Life and Thought of Michael Sattler* (Scottdale: Herald Press, 1984). Hardcover, viii, 260pp. ISBN 0-8361-1264-4
$10.00 U.S./$12.00 Canadian. Postage: $4.00 U.S./$5.00 Can.
[*First full-length biography of this Anabaptist leader and martyr*]

Pandora Press
51 Pandora Avenue N.
Kitchener, Ontario, Canada N2H 3C1
Tel./Fax: (519) 578-2381
E-mail: panpress@golden.net
Web site: www.pandorapress.com

Herald Press
616 Walnut Avenue
Scottdale, PA, U.S.A. 15683
Orders: (800) 245-7894
E-mail: hp@mph.org
Web site: www.mph.org